MYTHS AND REALITIES OF ACADEMIC ADMINISTRATION

MYTHS AND REALITIES OF ACADEMIC ADMINISTRATION

Patricia R. Plante
with
Robert L. Caret

378.11 P713

AMERICAN COUNCIL ON EDUCATION ☒ MACMILLAN PUBLISHING COMPANY
New York

COLLIER MACMILLAN PUBLISHERS
London

Macmillan Publishing Company
866 Third Avenue, New York, N.Y. 10022

Collier Macmillan Canada, Inc.

Library of Congress Catalog Card Number: 89-28183

Printed in the United States of America

printing number
1 2 3 4 5 6 7 8 9 10

Library of Congress Cataloging-in-Publication Data

Plante, Patricia R.
    Myths and realities of academic administration / Patricia R.
Plante, Robert L. Caret.
        p.   cm. — (American Council on Education/Macmillan series in
higher education)
    ISBN 0-02-897335-6
    1. College administrators—United States.   2. Universities and
colleges—United States—Administration.   I. Caret, Robert L.,
1947-   . II. Title. III. Series.
LB2341.P574   1989   89-28183
378.73—dc20   CIP

"I could have saved my life, she thought. But I was too weak, shackled by the wrong mythology."
                                        A Misalliance
                                        Anita Brookner

Contents

Preface

In an old Buster Keaton movie, described by Joseph Epstein in one of his collections of essays (*The Middle of My Tether*, W. W. Norton, New York, 1987, p. 212), Keaton decides to become a contestant on a radio amateur hour. In an effort to win a prize he chooses, in a madcap but characteristically deadpan manner, to display his talent at juggling. As he somberly keeps throwing balls up in the air, radio listeners, hearing only dead sound, pound and kick their Philco consoles, thinking their sets have suffered an unexpected death.

All academic administrators have upon occasion, but especially as they enter new and demanding positions, felt as if they were juggling balls that no one else could see; on other occasions they have feared that others were juggling balls they could not see—however energetically they banged on the old radio. One suspects that on both sets of occasions, their feelings were not so much a commentary on the challenges of a first- or second-year experience as on what many have come to expect of senior administrators in a contemporary college or university where the term *groves of academe*, with its suggestion of pastoral serenity and welcome shade, grows quainter by the year.

However, even in the strong glare of imagining comprehensive modern curricula, defending budgets before governing boards, shepherding building projects through city planning commissions, and mediating assorted serious and petty disputes—even under these potentially blinding conditions—one's vision should remain keen enough to examine the validity of certain myths about the life of an academic administrator.

Now, a myth (used here and throughout as a received idea containing some portion of truth) will often elicit two responses similar to those called forth by a cliché—be it a cliché phrase, a cliché decision, or a cliché life. One, we have grown accustomed to a myth and we are not at all certain that we want to devote the time necessary to develop an equally deep affection for any concept that has come to dislodge it. Two, though a myth, in the popular sense employed here, may not contain the whole truth—indeed, at times not even as much as a half-truth—it will nearly always contain some percentage of truth and any amount of truth is precious enough to attract its defenders. These two responses point, of course, to the central danger in a myth or a cliché: the temptation of being lured by one or the other or both to defer leading seriously examined professional lives.

Hence, while running the race it becomes important to save enough breath to huff and to puff and to blow the roof off, if not the house down, on at least some of the more widely and often repeated myths. Though their numbers are many, this work's purpose is to take down eight from bookshelves in administrative offices and to invite readers to appraise their worth.

However well prepared an administrator judges him- or herself to be, one suspects that most, in assuming for the first time the position of president, vice-president, dean, director, are poised to embrace without much thought any number of myths. For example, do senior administrators really experience a honeymoon period? Is it truly lonely at the top? Is an administrator apt to inherit untouchables? Will an administrator be drawn and quartered by conflicting constituencies? Is it due to a lack of will that an administrator cannot find a way? Are there occasions when an administrator must be less than truthful? Are the demands of managing and leading a modern college or university such that a senior administrator is forced to abandon a rigorous life of the mind? Will he or she then inevitably yearn to return to the classroom?

Myths large and small, light and dark, serious and frivolous, are strewn all over the office floors of experienced administrators. But few are bold enough to consign them to the archives, for in quiet moments of self-examination they admit that in the best of romantic traditions they find it difficult to say goodbye. The myths have lost their vigor and they do not in any sense count for very much any more except in this one way: they serve as reminders that at any given moment even experienced administrators may well replace them with myths of their own creation to satisfy a need to pursue an elusive order to which we are all perhaps unduly attracted.

Roland Barthes has written that "to interrogate mythology is to interrogate what had been in its time a fulfilled answer" (*The Responsibility of Forms*, Farrar, Straus and Giroux, New York, 1985, p. 68). "Fulfilled answers" are far removed from scientifically correct answers. There are, of course, no methodologies to "prove" or to "disprove" the myths discussed in the pages that follow. However, one can with profit come to certain conclusions about the wisdom of accepting them as inevitable, about the accuracy with which they reflect one's experience, and about the potential consequences of transmitting them unquestioned and whole.

In preparing this book, my colleague, Robert L. Caret, provost at Towson State University, and I agreed that I would do all the writing and that he would gather responses for those sections entitled, *Other Voices, Other Views*, which follow the essays in each chapter. This collecting of views was never intended as a scientific field study, but rather as an informal attempt to match the administrative experience of colleagues to the "wisdom" and "truth" of each of the myths under examination. The directions in the soliciting letter were simple: "Your response may be brief or long, theoretical or anecdotal. All we ask is that you comment on the 'truth' of the statement—on how closely your experience has come to approximating the conventionally accepted wisdom of the statement [myth]." One hundred twenty-six presidents, vice presidents, and deans from institutions large and small, from colleges and universities both public and private, and from virtually every state in the country shared two hundred nine commentaries. Some reflected on more than one of the suggested myths. Their views were not for attribution; their comments, except for the correcting of obvious typographical errors, the occasional clarification of a pronoun lost in space, and the elimination of unnecessary introductory phrases, were not edited. Some of the commentaries were reproduced in their entirety, some in part, some not at all. Those included in the exercise were chosen because the vision they expressed or their tone differed from the essay that preceded them and from one another. The order in which they appear is intended to fan discussion, even debate.

Patricia R. Plante
Portland, Maine

Acknowledgment

We wish to thank the one hundred twenty-six presidents, vice-presidents, and deans who commented on the myths examined in this work. Their generosity and their good-natured and sprightly replies have confirmed our belief that the serious demands of leading today's colleges and universities have damaged neither the courage nor the humor of many senior administrators.

Chapter 1

An Administrator Will Experience a Honeymoon

Depending on which "uncle" advises you, you have three or six or nine months to make significant changes on campus before the faculty begin to refer to the former regime as *la belle epoque*. The advice may well be sound in those very rare cases where the marriage follows an ardent courtship. However, most college and university administrators enter into an arranged union; few campuses during the selection process experience what French novels refer to as a *coup de foudre*. No one is struck by lightning. Some go-between of a search committee simply concludes, often with trepidation, that the match might lead to happiness and the chosen one agrees to the bond with enthusiasm, but with the knowledge that in an uncertain world many things break.

From that moment on, an administrator's every decision is a *vernissage*. Every decision is hung for every critic, on and off campus, trained and untrained, to evaluate and, above all, to interpret. And no decision made the first year is of passing interest—as it well might be in the third or fourth year by which time the administrator himself or herself has taken on some of the comfortable nature of a myth or cliché. In those early days, every word, every memo, every act, every smile or frown is interpreted and reinterpreted as an exercise in forecasting. Everyone from the president of the university senate to the president of the chamber of commerce becomes temporarily engaged in textual analysis. Even the knowledge that such close readings often distort perspective and may be as profitable as divining by examining the shoulder blades of sacrificial sheep deters only a few from becoming instant deconstructionists. Hence, though it is true that a carte blanche is stapled to the announcement of an administrator's appointment, one would be both prudent and wise to write on it with care, for nothing can be erased without leaving a smudge; and representatives of every constituency within and without the academy are, during the first year of an administrator's tenure, *not* lovers, *not* allies, *not* comrades, *not* mates, but above all explicators of text.

A simplified and shortened account of an adventure from the first season of one president's tenure may serve as illustration. His is an urban comprehensive university with an enrollment of about 10,000. Beneath the reasonably calm waters of collegial relationships that both faculty and administrators seek to cultivate between his institution and the state's land-grant university swims a giant-size tension. The president had barely unpacked his moving crates when this tension surfaced and leapt high into the air.

The leadership of the high-tech firms in the area wanted access to continuing education in electrical engineering without having to travel over a 100 miles to the land-grant school. In response to that need, this president's university sought to add an electrical engineering program in its college of applied sciences. Many within the college of engineering at the land-grant institution vehemently opposed the proposal as an added threat to their own very fine and nationally accredited program that, nevertheless, had been experiencing a decline in enrollment.

As a veteran of civil strife between urban comprehensive universities and land-grant institutions, the president was not unfamiliar with the tactics and rhetoric of such skirmishes, but was unprepared for the emotional depths from which this one sprang. In early fall a reporter from the

Chronicle of Higher Education was writing a story on the competition between land-grant universities and urban comprehensives, a competition that is now widespread and that some predict will become one of the central issues in higher education in the 1990s. The reporter asked for an interview with the president, and since this topic was of great interest to him, he agreed. The following paraphrases one of the reporter's questions and the president's answer:

QUESTION: What could be done to lessen the tension between flagship universities and the growing urban comprehensive universities?

ANSWER: Well, we might begin by ridding ourselves of seafaring metaphors that declare certain institutions to be favored over others.

In engaging in textual analysis of his own, The president could not have attracted more attention if he had dynamited the campanile at the very moment that its chimes rang out the first bars of the university's alumni song. The quote was clipped, stapled, arrowed, circled, underlined in multicolored ink, dragged through the local papers, and pulled out by its pinned-back ears at propitious moments in debates before the legislature and at hearings before the board of trustees. The new president was an outsider who did not understand the state's history or culture; he had clearly every intention of planning, if not the demise, the serious weakening of the land-grant institution; he had the lean and hungry look of the overly ambitious who hoped to transfer all engineering programs to his own pretentious campus.

While the interpretation of that one spontaneous sentence, intended to lighten but most certainly not to ridicule a weighty matter, differed from one campus to another within the system and from one part of the state to the other, the fact is that the explication of text led to a bazaar of conclusions regarding the direction that strategic planning for his institution was about to take and to a series of reviews regarding the very obvious flaws and strengths of his urban-influenced character.

One might find effective ways to reduce the tension associated with being transformed into a text that attracts interpreters, both trained and untrained, if all the critics belonged to the same school of criticism and cherished common aesthetic principles. Alas, this world too is imperfect and infinitely too complex to inspire handbooks. That the cafeteria pyrex coffee pot with a burnt-orange handle is a sign that the coffee therein is decaffeinated may be one of the few readings in an academic setting that does not call forth a challenge.

In the semeiotics of college and university presidencies, and in only slightly diminished forms in the semeiotics of vice-presidencies and deanships, both actions and words do indeed mean more than themselves. Presidents who attend every football game are not simply persons who enjoy football—a matter of no interest whatever. They are undoubtedly "good ol' persons" who can be counted on. What they can be counted on for is obscure, but that they can be is clear. Or presidents who attend every football game are perhaps individuals who are overly attracted to winning and may not be above sliding a card up their sleeve. They bear watching. Or, again, such presidents are indifferent to the well-documented corruption in intercollegiate sports. Or such presidents are more devoted to sports than to the fine arts. Well, do they attend every faculty concert? They find time to go to games, but no one has seen them at the series of lectures on the Gnostic gospels or the dramatic readings from Aristophanes. Each interpreter not only defends his or her interpretations with vigor but insists that his or her signs are the ones worthy of interpretation. Hence, the matter's complexity is not limited to the varied, even contradictory, readings, but is extended to disputes as to what signs are worthy of explication.

Faculty on one campus complained for years that its president, a young, energetic, ever-moving type, had a mind whose thoughts were permanently on the fluff cycle. He spent seven-day work weeks wooing the regional community and rarely engaged in questions of academic substance. Some grumbled that such leadership reflected values that were inimical to the mission of their university and would in time cause it to lose the respect of all but those who had only a superficial understanding of its distinguished purposes. All who failed to find beauty in the rhetoric of fund raising and in the rituals of legislative courting saw the president as simply using his office as an elevator to a higher floor with a better view. Others, however, maintained that as long as the provost had refined navigational skills, the president's comings and goings hardly mattered. Indeed, his enthusiastic luncheon hopping and all-too-obvious amassing of good will in the marketplace were too vulgar to be taken seriously by those old enough to have known dignified presidents and too remote to be attended to by those young enough to be charting careers.

Predictably, the search committee named to recommend his successor were lobbied heavily and successfully to bring to the institution someone whose style differed in many if not all respects from that of this one-minute manager. Hence, into the office stepped a middle-aged, sleepy-eyed, somewhat rumpled intellectual. This former vice-president for academic affairs, after very few tentative and unsuccessful forays into the pin-striped competitive business community and the cloak-and-dagger halls of the legislature, showed a marked preference for a rocking chair near the academic hearth. In a matter of months, this newly appointed president was accused by the critics who had ignored the high-profile style of his predecessor of exhibiting signs worth studying. No administrator should meddle with impunity in matters that were the appropriate concern of faculty. The distribution requirements had been carefully negotiated over a long period of time and were defensible, thank you very much. Who was this man to question the curriculum when he himself had not published a word in his field in sixteen years? Some interpreters began to detect signs of a mind whose thoughts were on no cycle at all. Meanwhile the detractors of the previous cultivator of charisma saw no reason to become alarmed. Without going to the extreme of defending the new president's attempted involvement in matters intellectual, they dismissed his attempts as no more than a desire to seek rapprochement with the faculty and students. Besides, no one, not even a president, moves a stick of furniture in the house of intellect without the permission of the faculty. Clearly these presidential signs were not worth the time to interpret.

The house into which a new president carries his or her books has seen previous occupants, and the spectators who watch the movers come and go are understandably inclined to gather notes for comparative studies on everything from taste in china and crystal to precision in the use of language to genuineness in professed dedication to the institution. These comparatists have formed individualized versions of an ideal leader for their institution and of an ideal relationship between that leader and themselves.

The somewhat gentle but preliminary assessments come almost immediately. "Well, he certainly doesn't have the presence of good old Sam." Or "It's apparent that she belongs to the new breed that cultivates distance. She may get more distance than she bargained for." Or "A bit serious, don't you think? We're going to miss Sam's wit. But, then again, we may not have to endure his puns." Or "Well, one can hope that, unlike Sam, she's read the books that fill the shelves in that study."

Many who had grown tired of trying to improve the previous president are revivified by the possibility that the new one will demonstrate characteristics that they wish the previous tenant had shown. In a world where it never rains on parades, the previous president had been blunt and the new one will be diplomatic; the previous one had been prosaic and the new one will be eloquent; the previous one had managed details poorly and the new one will manage them well. Note, of course, that while these strengths are installed in the presidential manse, the previous president's virtues remain ensconced in the front parlor. Hence, if the previous president had been strong in the community and weak on campus, the new one is expected to be strong both in the community and on the campus. There is rarely serious talk of substituting one strength for another. This world view is optimistic, linear, and progressive: just as contemporary scholarship builds on the discoveries and insights of the past, the emotional expectation, if not the reasoned one, is that the new president will somehow add but not subtract from the accumulated wisdom and arts and skills of all his or her predecessors.

Once a campus returns, with various degrees of grace, to an acceptance of an inevitably imperfect world, its faculty, staff, students, and alumni, will also return to debating the merits of one presidential style over another. And while there may well be as many views on the matter as there are debaters, all will accept one proposition: a campus must never be embarrassed by its president. And in the academy, the sin against the Holy Ghost is intellectual. Of course, one has a right to expect honesty, and fair play, and dedication, and close effective attention to detail, and much more, but above all one has a right to expect a level of discourse that is in keeping with the lofty mission of a university.

One unfortunate president, so the story is told, never recovered from having referred to George Eliot as "he" in an early talk to the assembled faculty. One vice-president for development earned the mistrust of faculty and students alike at her first appearance in the academic senate by delivering announcements and comments that were considered linguistic trailblazers: words strung together in such a way as to defy the understanding of even the most attentive listeners. Senior-level administrators are not expected to advance the frontiers of immunology, but they are expected to know that the frontiers exist. Senior-level administrators are not frowned upon for not composing contemporary operas, but they are frowned upon for referring to Philip Glass as a third baseman with the Oakland A's. One should not be encouraged to create metaphors from the biological sciences if one has read no biology since high school, for an authentic voice is a respected voice. However, an "aw shucks" voice will not do, and an important thing to remember is that all but the comatose on campus are particularly eager to write a review of that voice upon first hearing.

To jump from leading and managing a firm that sells copying machines to one that sells pocket cellular telephones is not much of a leap and takes relatively little training. However, it takes a significant part of a lifetime to prepare for effective senior-level academic management and leadership, and the halls are filled with critics who are eager and curious to see whether the new person does as well or better than the chemist or the anthropologist or the city manager or the fund raiser who preceded him or her. Hence, campuses harbor not only explicators of texts, but comparatists of texts.

That which inspires in explicators/comparatists this serious interest in any newly arrived senior-level administrator is most certainly, at least in part, the predilection for the safeguarding of one's own future. Half the academic community feels that it was understood and appreciated by the previous president or vice-president or dean, and fear that the new point person may not possess the same perspicacity and good taste; the other half of the academic community is certain that the previous title holder was too myopic to appreciate true worth and is hoping that the replacement is capable of finer-honed judgments. The tests administered to the newly arrived administrator will take both simple and rococo forms, but many will volunteer to grade them.

Among the most common of these examinations are the following: one, "all eyes are upon you"; two, "we had been led to believe"; and, three, "you will destroy." The structure of the tests appropriate the lines characteristic of the style of a campus's faculty and staff leadership, but regardless of the method of inquiry, the intent is universal: the time has come to hug the plate and to see what control this pitcher brings to the mound.

All Eyes Are upon You

Professor Y, a senior member of the department of English, having convinced himself that he is pure of heart and purpose, asks to see the newly appointed dean in order to give her a map pinpointing the location of a deadly mine that has been laid on the terrain she is preparing to cross. It is "I thought you should know" hour. Professor X, whose undeniable erudition has blinded previous administrators, has never had any but his own welfare as a goal. Now he seeks a renewed term as department head and all English professors as well as many of their colleagues in neighboring departments are crowded in the crow's nest standing watch to spot the new dean's judgment of character. Professor Y would never have come to see the dean if he had not wished her to succeed; it is not a question of loving Professor X less, but of loving the institution more. Within days, Professor X, equally persuaded that he is without a trace of guile, takes the time away from his heavy responsibilities to brief the dean on the history of a department that for years has had to defend itself against the sabotaging efforts of Professor Y whose pathological state of mind includes a desire to record the failure of all deans. All eyes are upon the dean, for an administrator who cannot see through the wiles of a Professor Y is perhaps without the experience needed to lead a college of arts and sciences. Professor X stands ready to support the dean in all ways this side of honesty. After all, no newcomer, however skillful and talented, can hope to understand an institution within a short period of time without the aid of those who have loved it for years.

We Had All Been Led to Believe

An ambassadorial delegation of the faculty senate requests an hour with the newly appointed president of the university to describe certain values that have always informed a campus where they wish him to prosper and grow old. This comprehensive university has always prized and rewarded excellence in teaching and has always been skeptical of the claim that research necessarily contributed to it in any significant way. Why, they could cite examples of young professors who had been denied tenure because their absorption in scholarship had led to the neglect of their teaching. Now, the presi-

dent in forums here and there seems to be referring to scholarship and research in ways that have ignited the anxiety of
some members of the older faculty who care deeply about
the values of this institution. Of course, they may have mis-
understood, and an unambiguous statement from the president's office would put the matter to rest. They are aware
that a group of young scholars on campus are unsympathetic
to their view, but the president would be wise to listen atten-
tively to those who have been working in the fields for years
and who know what will grow there. Furthermore, they had
been led to believe by the presidential search committee that
the president and the university were meant for each other
precisely because their values were identical. It would be
disappointing, indeed, to discover that they had been mis-
led. As a matter of record, it might be more than disappointing; it might be disruptive. And, above all, what they seek
and what they are certain the newly arrived president seeks
are harmonious relations during what everyone hopes will
be for him a long and successful administrative tenure. Of
course, the future is always uncertain, is it not?

You Will Destroy

The president of the alumni association, with a confident
and proprietary walk, strides into the office of the vice-president for development before the latter has even hung his
prints on his new office walls. People should understand one
another from the beginning. He is in business and has little
patience with the processes of the academy, but when in
Rome and all that. He will support the new V.P., no questions asked. That is the sort of person he is. There is just one
thing that would send everybody off on a very bumpy ride:
the staff person who heads the alumni office has confided
that the new vice-president's initiatory questions about the
past discharging of her responsibilities seemed to be critical
and overly intrusive. He is certain that her fears are the result of a misunderstanding. He has been a leading force in
the alumni association for twenty years during which that

staff person has been right there working cooperatively with him. The institution owes her and he has become very protective of her—for the sake of the future of the university and the association. But, listen, the vice-president has come highly recommended; he trusts him to see the whole picture. Indeed, he is so enthusiastic about his appointment that he and all the important contacts he has made throughout the region are there just waiting to be asked to help the vice-president in all his development efforts. He has no intention of limiting himself to working on the annual alumni fund. In sum, he is pleased that they had this little talk, for getting started on the right foot is important to winning any race. Besides, he has succeeded in business in part because he is a confident judge of character and he can tell that this vice-president is a winner of races.

That such common conditions and likely happenings as those described above should bring immediately to anyone's mind the euphoria of a honeymoon is evidence of either an idiosyncratic definition of sweetness and harmony or of a non-traditional experience in the first month of marriage. Donald Barthelme ends one of his short stories by having the narrator look out the window at neighbors who always eat breakfast by candlelight. He has never been able to figure out whether they are terminally romantic or are trying to save electricity. Perhaps those who compare a senior-level administrator's initiatory period to a honeymoon are simply giving signs of a romantic turn of mind. But, then again, they might be quite practically conserving energy for the day when cold winds really rattle the shutters.

OTHER VOICES, OTHER VIEWS

From the President of a Private University:

My own experiences suggest that a time of change, if properly prepared for, can be a moment for institutional self-appraisal and for the encouragement of new enthusiasm about the common task. If the new president is given a fair amount of discretion, then a number of human dynamics can be tapped into which can make those at lower levels of administration and other participants in the university community feel that they have a share in shaping the institution's future. In that sense, an administrator will experience a honeymoon. There is a certain span of time at the beginning of a new administration when everybody is getting his or her clues about visions and procedures that will prevail in the years ahead. Since I was promoted from within, I had the advantage of being a known quantity and also with being personally familiar with the majority of individuals with whom I would be in most frequent contact.

As I look at other institutions, I can think of administrators who would be under the gun right from the start. This would include those entrusted with the task of paring away certain units of the university or freezing salaries or enforcing more rigorous standards for hiring and promotion. None of these factors existed in my situation so I have not felt the kind of emotional pressure that some other administrators have faced.

From the Academic Vice-President of a Private College:

The length of the honeymoon of the administrator is precisely proportional to the length of time it takes the faculty to realize that the new spouse is essentially no different from the old. Such cold light descends when the new administrator reveals he or she is not the mirror image of the new partner and fails to reflect each smile, each mood, each desire, each twinkle, and each budgeting priority.

The administrator's honeymoon may last an hour, a day, a month, but no longer than the next phase of the financial cycle. At the end of the honeymoon, alone at the table facing a cold meal, the administrator may comfort himself or herself, as I have done, by contemplating the truth enshrined on a plaque in my mother-in-law's kitchen: Kissing Don't Last; Good Cooking Do.

From the President of a Community College:

We have, generally, upon assuming a new position, a period of grace. People are evaluating us, probing, attempting to determine our values and style. As these become increasingly clear, the honeymoon gives way to what I call "Phase 1 acceptance." This is an early period in your tenure in which various constituencies start either to work with you, against you, or ignore you. You still have a lot of leeway. It generally takes a series of "tests" by individuals and constituents before they firm up their conclusions about what you do and how you do it.

Senior administrators are judged differently by each individual in the institution: whether or not you are effective depends, in their respective eyes, on whether you have fulfilled their respective expectations. This can also extend to groups. Given our present societal preoccupation with individual rights as against shared responsibility, it is difficult for an administrator to call upon shared values in an organizational culture as a basis for his or her being judged.

The honeymoon ends when people feel they know what you are going to do and how you are going to do it. It ends when your predictability diminishes their hope.

From the President of a Public University:

Most people within higher education are civil and inclined to give newcomers a chance. Every campus has a few truly destructive individuals who are exceptions, but, at least, at the beginning of a tenure, these voices will not predominate. The length of the honeymoon will be determined by an administrator's skill and/or the presence/absence of critically divisive issues. Nevertheless, in my experience on numerous campuses, we are all given a fair chance except in isolated instances, usually at the departmental level, where previously existing internal divisions make success almost impossible.

From the Dean of a School of Art of a Private University:

I share your interest in the folklore of administration which has (selectively) been defined as everything from "institutional memory" to policy. . . . Having served at two quite different institutions (at a large public university where in effect I came out of the family and at a large private university in which deans are perceived as, and expected to be, deans of faculty rather than of administration), I have never experienced the "honeymoon syndrome." Maybe it all depends on who you marry.

For what it's worth I give you the following which are probably not quite in the myth category, but do have something to recommend them as guidance for administrators.

——Nobody wants to hear about labor pains, they only want to see the baby. *Johnny Sain, Pitching Coach of the Detroit Tigers.*

——Any manager that can't get along with a .400 hitter is crazy. *Joe McCarthy, Manager of the New York Yankees.*

——Never mistake asthma for passion. *Anonymous.*

From the Provost of a Private University:

Anyone who can't look good and receive reasonably gentle treatment for at least a few months is probably too dumb to make it for the long haul. During the honeymoon, the bride or groom is praised for the "breath of fresh air" he or she brings to the academy and even forgiven for less than mortal sins. But I've rarely seen honeymoon last longer than six months or so before the natural hatred of "the administration" (including the former breath of fresh air) sets in. The honeymoon is renewed at retirement when for a few months one could be led to believe that brilliance reigned.

From the Provost of a Public University:

After moving into several academic administrative positions over a seventeen-year period, I have concluded that the "honeymoon" myth is indeed a myth. While there may well be a brief period of particular good will toward the new incumbent, there is also an onrush of people whose pet projects or wishes were turned down by the predecessor and who hope the new incumbent will make a different decision.

People are especially nice when they are seeking something for the first time from a new administrator, but academics quickly revert to form—they know that their own position is correct and that if the answer is no, the administrator is simply not doing his job well.

If they are charitable, they may assume that external constraints keep the administrator from meeting the faculty member's request, but more often, I'm afraid, they simply assume that another administrator is making a bad job of it.

Administrators should not rely on "honeymoons" but rather upon sound principles and good evidence to support their decisions.

From the Provost and Dean of a Public University:

Some people have the talent of being able to take time to learn the "corporate culture," get to know the players and the problems, build a support team, get a capital campaign planned, and generate statewide visibility before they get in any trouble with their faculty or board. Not me! I've always had the bad habit of jumping right in, making budget changes, cleaning house, and making a powerful enemy within a short time after taking office. I figure life's too short not to have fun.

From the Dean of a Branch Campus of a Public University:

Sometimes a belief in a honeymoon can affect you though you do not profess a belief in that myth. I was one of two finalists for the provost's position at ____ some years ago. The president at the time telephoned me to tell me that he had chosen the other candidate. One of his reasons: "If I picked you, I wouldn't have a honeymoon."

From the President of a Public University:

I am inclined to think that there is some small shred of truth in this statement [myth], but it's not very significant. I am now in my third position in which I have served as a chief executive officer for an institution or a system; therefore, I have had some direct opportunity to determine whether or not there is a "honeymoon" case.

It is likely that in most instances a new chief administrator would be given a slight "honeymoon" that will be nothing more than receiving the benefit of the doubt for the first few months. That will be the extent of it. It is probably also true that the immediate supervisor (whether that be a governing board, coordinating board, or an individual) would tend to be "nice" to the new person on the job for at least a little while. Anyone who believes, however, that so-called honeymoon is guaranteed or that it will last for at least a year is kidding himself. Generally speaking, it will last until the first major problem arises and that's the end of it.

From the Dean of a College of Education at a Public University:

There is no such thing as a honeymoon period! The instant a new administrator takes his or her new office, the previously deprived descend on the new possibilities they perceive. When the new administrator does not react to their delayed wishes—nothing has changed.

From the Vice-President for Academic Affairs at a Public University:

To use Goffman's notion of "front stage," the new administrator may be unaware of the extent to which he or she is "on stage," and that judgments are being made, and made early regarding his or her initial performance. Others' perceptions are being shaped during this early period, and if an administrator is operating under the assumption that he or she has a "honeymoon," he or she may well be engaging in substantial self-deception that could function to endanger his or her success as time progresses in the position. The "honeymoon myth" emerges because people are unusually friendly and the body language, etc., is perceived as the foundation for the establishment of friendship when in fact the interactions are based far more on assessment than on a desire for friendship. It is the new administrator's desire for friendship that may deceive him or her, causing needless self-disclosure and vulnerability during the early weeks and months.

From the Provost of a Public University:

A honeymoon assumes a wedding at which both parties agree to love, honor, and cherish each other. It is not clear that faculty are always willing to make this commitment to a new administrator.

In more elegant parlance, a honeymoon is usually referred to as a wedding trip. Perhaps if the new administrator and the faculty could take a trip together at the outset, things might get off to a better start.

From the Academic Vice-President and Acting President of a Public College:

All of my advancement has been at the same institution. Far from my being extended a honeymoon, I have generally been expected to immediately, and finally, "get the job done right." Individuals on campus seem to gain an intuitive understanding of how I would handle any given situation, based on observation of my past behavior, and they are impatient if issues are not resolved with great dispatch. It is assumed that I know all of the players intimately and will be able to accomplish miracles in changing attitudes and positions in hours or days.

I must assume that when moving to another institution there will be a period in which the new administrator and the campus community feel each other out. This will, of course, look as if it is a honeymoon. In reality, it will only apply to those issues which are not critical to the operation of the institution and which are not of critical importance to any segment of the community. Administrators come and go, but the institution must continue to function and decisions must be made. If the decisions are not popular, the administrator will be so informed (and blamed) whether new on the scene or not.

From the Academic Vice-President of a Private College:

It seems to me the situation is not unlike the honeymoon of newlyweds. The bliss continues until she squeezes the toothpaste tube the wrong way or fails to wipe out the wash basin frequently enough (two of my wife's obvious shortcomings) or he persists in dropping his shoes wherever he happens to be when he tires of wearing them or eats pickled herring before bedtime (two matters that have been brought to my attention). There is a high probability that the length of the honeymoon and the frequency with which provocative incidents arise are inversely related.

From the Dean of the College of Arts and Sciences of a Public University:

The distal end of the process may be more certain (i.e., sooner or later, the administrator will experience a divorce, amicable or otherwise!). The quality of the honeymoon, if any, depends very much upon the circumstances leading up to the administrator's appointment. One may also ask, "A honeymoon with whom?" There are a lot of partners to this marriage. Since the higher administration (or the board) almost always selects a candidate who seems to suit their needs, the honeymoon is most likely to occur between the appointee and his organizational superiors. But even here there are questions. Was the predecessor a well-loved "old boy" who finally decided to retire, despite the protestations of the board and senior administrators? Can any mortal live up to the legacy? Were these parties in full agreement about the replacement?

From the faculty perspective, a new administrator is always a two-edged sword, offering both renewed hope for leadership in areas that have been neglected and the potential for oppression. Faculty thus hope for the best but remain cautious about the new administrator's ability to appreciate and work constructively with the institution's particular traditions and culture.

All things considered, the more accurate statement may be: "A new administrator will be given enough rope."

Chapter 2

An Administrator Will Lead a Hyperkinetic Life

Some medical researchers postulate that under certain conditions a person might become chemically addicted to the adrenalin produced by his or her own body. Addiction in such cases would quite literally resemble addiction to any other substance such as nicotine or cocaine. Twenty-five years ago in *The Painted Bird*, the novelist Jersy Kosinski described this phenomenon in unforgettable scenes depicting the trials of a child who had been separated from his parents during World War II. After years of living on the qui vive, of existing in a state of heightened consciousness in order to survive the brutality of bestial peasants in Eastern Europe, he finds the brawls and petty cruelties of life in a post-war orphanage to make for penny ante days.

He begins deliberately to court a danger that produces the "highs" to which he had become addicted. Mornings and evenings a train passes close by the orphanage. A few minutes before the arrival of the train, he puts on a show for awe-struck children from nearby settlements by lying face down between the tracks to wait for the hot breath of the train furnace to sweep over him and for the great engine to roll furiously over his back. At that moment he feels intensely alive. "In the moments between the passing of the locomotive and the last car I felt within me life in a form as pure as milk carefully strained through a cloth" (*The Painted Bird*, Modern Library, New York, 1965, p. 218).

In reduced forms, we have all experienced both the heightened periods of intense and focused concentration and the "letting go" that follows. In happenings as widely diverse as writing books and waging political campaigns, when the entrance to one's attention is locked to everything but that which adds a paragraph or brings in a vote, we have known the attractions and joys of all-consuming encounters. We have also known the dispersal of energies, the vague dissatisfaction, and the sense of loss that follow the completion of even worthy books and successful campaigns. And thus, on days when the world seems to be too much with us and we know it is time to appropriate some silence even from loud inner voices, we may in some subterranean part of the mind fear that detached from causes, projects, and plans, the "I" might meet with emptiness. Having known both the pressure and the weight of time, we may have subconsciously concluded that bearing the first was less demanding than lifting the second.

Perhaps in an effort to ward off any pause "between the heaves of storms" an administrator launches project 12 before project 11 is barely in orbit in an attempt to maintain what few now regard as an unbecoming pace. Now on campuses of a certain size at least, every day can provide electrifying moments for an administrator who remains alert to them. The walls of universities in all but small backwater junctions vibrate with the potential for crisis management, and an imaginative administrator's day is never done. Thanks in part to the frenzied tempo often induced by his or her own needs to be up and doing, a contemporary administrator on a contemporary campus need never pause and run the risk of enduring the search for meaning. Promoting the growth of a university that has gone over the wall and is now engaged in extensive collaboration with government and business can easily become the administrator's book without epilogue, the campaign without end. And, paradoxically, the welcome assurance that the finish line will never be crossed is the very condition that frees many an administrator to run ever faster.

The manifestations of this addiction to the "runner's high" are everywhere. Presidents, vice-presidents and deans, clutching tightly their attaché cases, return from national conferences wide-eyed with undisguised anxiety after having learned that colleagues are running well in races where they themselves would likely be eliminated in preliminary heats. One campus, with a president given to returning from such meetings with an impossibly long list of projects and pretentious plans that if ever completed by others would win her medals, has quite cynically, but without malice aforethought, fallen into a pattern of polite passive resistance. Since, in this instance, the president attends many meetings and in her agitated state forgets the lists of yesteryear, the institution transcends her lack of discipline and does reasonably well.

Unquestionably, one sign of the hyperkinetic syndrome is the tendency of many administrators to dig holes under the fences that confine them to a focused mission. Why should we not prepare ourselves to offer doctoral programs? If North Carolina has a bio-tech park, why should we not have one also? Centers of Excellence? But of course. Retraining of displaced workers? Absolutely. Collaborative efforts with the public school system? Continuing education for computer scientists? Programs for the growth management of cities? For child care? Without a doubt. Exchange agreements with mainland China? Poland? Russia? Pourquoi-pas? Indeed, why should we not be the first to establish one with Burma? Ah, to be the first. To that chord, every heart quickens.

To suggest that the only motivation for this hyperactivity is nothing more elevated than a desire to show the sleepy world what an athletic, risk-taking, charismatic entrepreneur can do would be manifestly unfair. Many who have become addicted to such behavior and professional way of life sincerely seek to serve both their institution and the community at large. However, intentions, pure though they be, contribute very little to the successful end of the story.

To imply that in displaying this hyperactivity, the academic administrator outruns his time and place would be equally unjust. The close observer of social trends, John Naisbitt, has informed us that Americans have in the past fifteen years dramatically reduced their leisure time. In 1987, the American "average worker's spare time totaled 16.6 hours a week, down from 26.2 hours in 1973. Meanwhile the work week expanded to 46.8 hours, six hours more than 15 years ago. . . . Two- and three-week vacations are vanishing" (John Naisbitt, *Trend Letter*, October 27, 1988, p. 6). Indeed, observant entrepreneurs who have assessed the condition of both the track and the runners have set up successful companies to perform services that can still elicit a shake of the head in the provinces. These companies will organize everything from your garage and closets to your leisure time. One, New York's Strand Book Store, will even set up a library for your home—though how those who cannot find the time to collect their own books will find the time to read them is a conundrum for retirement years.

However, the hyperkinetic syndrome manifests itself in the academy in its own idiosyncratic and additional ways. The academic land is alive with the sound of buzz words that rarely live to celebrate their fifth birthday. Alert administrators who number crunch so as to watch the bottom line; who access information so as to put together appropriate packages; who respect both input and output so as to understand the infrastructure; who position their institutions to provide a value added education can now jump through windows of opportunity—providing, of course, that they interface well and know how to have a nice day. With little additional effort, they can also attend professional seminars for which few, even the director, have had time to prepare. They can sit on boards to read many a superficially reasoned and poorly written proposal. They can watch or join harried "facilitators" who facilitate nothing; confused leaders return from whence they had begun; planners turn time and time again to lecturers whose thinking and writing are done on Chief-

tains and 747's and in whose work one can detect muddied
coffee stains and air pockets. Indeed, one academic jet setter,
embarrassed by his rambling, trivial approach to important
matters in a commencement address, excused himself at the
end of the ceremony on the grounds that he had given seven
graduation addresses in two weeks.

The poor owl of a mind flies, now in this direction, now
in the other, in an attempt to escape the dangers of a deceler-
ated pace. And the academic administrator who seeks ever
greater speed will likely turn to high technology for impres-
sive and reliable assistance. Your mother, bless her good and
simple heart, was wrong: you most certainly can do more
than one thing at once. And, furthermore, you can live to
take pride in so doing and to describe the adventures in si-
multaneity to colleagues while shaking your blow-dry hair-
cut in awe at all you are able to do without much thought.
You can, for instance, easily carry on a telephone conversation while reading a report while watching the proceedings
of a conference prerecorded on your V.C.R. With the help
of a laser printer, a cellular car phone, a portable phone, a
dictaphone, a fax machine, interactive television, a portable
computer, a modem, a Walkman, and an answering machine, you can plot a Big Mac life that will take you from
indoor to outdoor running tracks with nary a pause. It is
multi-channel fiber optic brain-time everywhere but Lake
Wobegon.

Among the other manifestations of this addiction to
days of cyclone rides is the search for the "right contacts"—
individuals who might be cultivated to help an institution
rise above the level of its competitors. An adept hunter finds
them everywhere: on the top floor of bank buildings, in the
foyers of symphony halls, in the back rooms of automobile
dealerships, in the infirmaries of nursing homes. He or she
will collect a check here, a favor there, a barrel of goodwill
elsewhere. But the true purpose of the sport is to bag and to
mount the big trophy. "Don't lose your time with that one,
he's without real influence." "Send your assistant; there's no
real money there." A president may not even wince before a

vulgarity that urges him to court someone who is lonely and without "anyone to leave it to."

In a brilliant scene in *To Jerusalem and Back*, Saul Bellow captures the lines and hues of this compelling drive to make the meta-contact, the contact to end all contacts. At a White House reception Bellow introduces his wife to Hubert Humphrey who shakes their hands. "But he was in one of his public states. The fit was on him. He couldn't bear to be confined to the two of us. He was looking for someone more suitable, for the most suitable encounter, the one it could be death to miss. He was gripped by an all but demonic desire for the optimum encounter" (Viking Press, New York, 1976, p. 31). This elusive quarry, the most suitable encounter, is out there eating an hors d'oeuvre at the very next reception or sipping warm chardonnay at the very next conference. Direct your eye above the left shoulder of your future mini-encounters and scan the room as you chitchat. Surely, it is not too much to ask you to do but two things at once.

To dismiss this high-energy activist administrative mode as devoid of merit would be both simplistic and naive. A modern university is not a monastery dedicated solely to the preservation of the contemplative life. Few would consider the academic world's return to a posture of isolationism to be either practical or desirable. And only those same few might suggest that a college or university's mission need never be reexamined, redefined, and updated. Cassandras have muffled their wailing against the evils of high technology and only a curmudgeon here and there nurses a grudge against P.C.s. Of course, good planning calls for a university's openness to change—at times even of its traditional mission. Of course, technology that frees us from menial tasks and treats us to the gift of time should be welcomed. Of course, leaders both within and without the academy should be encouraged to collaborate in promoting the intellectual life of the nation.

At every intersection, however swings a flashing red light. The high-speed activist mode of administration carries with it dangers that can only be eluded if studied and understood. Two of the most serious and most threatening are the promotion of disorder and the fostering of anti-intellectualism in institutions whose common mission is the eradication of both.

The president referred to above who returned from field trips carrying specimens of activities conducted on other campuses that she wished were duplicated on her own never attempted to fold these activities into a well-thought-out plan of the whole. She viewed herself as a scatterer of seeds, her metaphor of choice, and upon occasion a sycophantic dean or chair would water them. The trouble, which the thoughtful foresaw, was that the campus would come upon squashes in the petunia beds. The thoughtful had also quickly come to note that the produce displayed would be as much of a surprise to the president as to anyone else because by harvest time she was off very busily scattering seeds in another more-or-less stony patch.

Signs of educational philosophies reduced to forms of marketing have multiplied and the experienced can bear witness to their blight across the landscape. Composites of those whose M.O.s are the "putting together of packages" are easily imagined. An academic vice-president whose ecclesiastical manner, down to the tonsured head, downcast eyes, and ascetic thinness, disguises a fierce ambition and a fibrillating heart arrives on campus at the dawn of a new academic year. He had left a small, homogeneous, liberal arts college, too remote to showcase his talents, to work among the hordes of holy writ in an urban comprehensive university. Determined to bring intellectual happiness to others at whatever cost to their own needs and convenience, he sets out to improve if not to reform the university.

He has read his journals; he has attended his conferences; he has heard the themes repeated in the lounges of Sheratons and Hiltons. His mind filled with undigested derivative thoughts, he is armed; he is ready. To begin with, his university will design a core curriculum worthy of notice, a core curriculum to end all debates about core curricula. Undeterred by a sleepy and unsophisticated office of institutional research, by a president whose upcoming retirement few are apt to notice, by a superficial knowledge of both his faculty's and his students' strengths and weaknesses, and, above all, by his own lack of convictions about the intellectual life most worth leading, he charges one committee after another with vaguely articulated missions.

In a flash, faculty who are not in class or who have not managed to hide find themselves closeted in meetings that are called in such rapid succession that no gap for reflection is allowed to peep between them. Meanwhile, gentle reader, our hero whose agenda is long seeks early closure on this, his matter of top priority. He prods, he pushes, and he pulls, guarding against any show of impatience, but letting both the board of trustees and the chamber of commerce know that his is an institution that has been awakened. His laser printer whirs, his modem hums, and his lap-top bounces on the back seat of his car as he travels between home and office.

The vice-president in a matter of weeks has created a climate where many are engaged in competitive feats of labor and speed. The favored greeting of the day has become, "How late did your sub-committee work last night?" However, what had begun as a good-natured and hopeful desire to cooperate with a leadership that seemed eager to ask questions that needed asking, turns in less than one term into short-tempered rebellion against an unfitting and unbecoming pace that short circuits deliberation, meditation, and judiciousness.

One can easily predict any number of endings, all of them leading to varied degrees of intellectual disorder. Perhaps the rebellion is so severe as to elicit a vote of no confidence in the vice-president and to sustain a mood on campus that militates against a reexamination of the core curriculum for some time to come. Or the rebellion takes the form of a confusion and discouragement so deep as to lead to a temporary moral forfeiting of the game whereupon the newly structured core curriculum remains erect until the judgmental scrutiny of a rested and reinvigorated faculty or a serious and demanding student body topples it. Or, again, the rebellion is so uncoordinated and so ineffectual that a

superficial core curriculum that never really addresses the
issue of the knowledge most worth having remains in place
for years, cheating thousands of students of an intellectual
growth that might have been theirs. An epilogue to this third
ending has the vice-president attaché case bulging with educational jargon, delivering papers that share with colleagues
the ways and means of bringing about needed change.

In the world of buying and selling, in the world of building and demolishing, in the world of acquiring and divest-
ing, Aesop (and LaFontaine after him) was mistaken: the
gifts of the hare are to be preferred to those of the tortoise.
Everyone knows that certain rewards do go to the swift.
However, the rewards of academicians differ from those of
arbitragers, and the means of achieving them carry their
own suitable and distinct tempo. Additionally, the notion of
swiftness itself has always projected in the intellectual world
its own very special connotation—a connotation, in its ideal
form, quite apart from that of besting others and winning
races. Indeed, it is a connotation of unworldly fleetness of
mind that is even unaware of the concept of fleetness of foot
and that accounts in part for amused fondness for stories of
savants who live in atmospheres so rarefied as to preclude
distractions that afflict the ordinary. The poet Delmore
Schwartz tells us that Alfred North Whitehead was in the
midst of advising students to read a particular philosopher
"with a grain of . . . a grain of . . ."; Schwartz came to his
assistance with "Of salt, Professor Whitehead?" and Whitehead said he was sure it was a mineral. From this, one cherishes academe's version of swiftness and hopes that worldliness will never take it from us (James Atlas, *Delmore
Schwartz*, Harcourt Brace Jovanovich, New York, p. 80).

It is one thing, praiseworthy and necessary, to provide
leadership that encourages constant self-renewal and openness to change, and quite another to launch multiple ambitious projects without regard for the mission, history, and
resources of an institution that should nurture ambitions
that rise above marketing itself as a place on the move. To
have an open mind is not to have an empty one. To move
for the sake of movement, for the sake of appearing to be

responsive to all constituents, for the sake of impressing onlookers with one's drive and flexibility, is to encourage a superficiality that masks disorder. A hyperventilation style of
administration invites initiatives that are poorly planned,
indifferently executed, and rarely assessed, for the motivating urge is to reach out for the excitement and romance of
perpetual beginnings. In time, a senior-level administrator
who cultivates that style runs the risk of commandeering the
voyage of an Athenian trireme with a broken compass and
three levels of entangled oars.

To accuse the hyperkinetic academic administrative
style of sanctioning anti-intellectualism, albeit unintention-
ally, is a serious charge that can be supported. While the
methodologies of all disciplines impress upon university students the need for painstaking analysis and for conscientious
synthesis, while these methodologies convince them of the
importance and beauty of imaginative thought and language, some academic administrators adopt a leadership
style that makes for careless decision making and thought-
less speaking and writing. Judiciousness unless instanta-
neous is dismissed as poky, for the medium is the message.
Fire the blazing fast ball via electronic mail and no one will
notice, let alone care, that it is out of the strike zone.

Superficial studies point to what everyone has long
known; addresses repeat information that everyone has often heard; professional journals print essays that everyone
could have written. The researchers, the speakers, and the
authors are running to their next photo opportunity. And,
ironically, the time they save by running is never their own.

Certain places, certain times endanger a life of reflection, a life of the mind. But surely the university in America
at the end of this century is not one of them and to make it
so is to invent conditions to meet one's own psychological
needs. The Israeli writer Avraham. B. Yehoshua explained
in an interview some years ago that the inescapable preoccupation with political questions in Israel engaged one without
end so that nothing was left, spiritually, for other things.
"Nor can you attain the true solitude that is a condition and
prerequisite of creation, the source and its strength." He said

that under such circumstances "you live the moment, without any perspective, but you cannot break free of the moment, forget the moment" (*Unease in Zion*, edited by Ehud ben Ezer, Quadrangle/New York Times Book Company, New York, 1974, pp. 337–38).

Senior academic administrators who, in imitation of tycoon developers and media moguls, cannot break free of the moment will not in the long run inspire confidence. Indeed, we have all witnessed cases of their calling forth barely concealed derision for a style that is out of keeping with the traditional values of the academy.

Those who would claim that a flash-dance style of administration, though in opposition to a university pace that is scholarly, is nevertheless the only one possible in an imperfect world are simply mistake. Presidents, vice-presidents, and deans, collectively, can set the standards for themselves; they are capable of determining a pace that supports modes of behavior that make room for thought, for meditation, for reflection. What if they walked off the field and refused to play? What if they posted placards in their studies thanking people for not installing modems? What if every Wednesday evening they read Montaigne and listened to Mozart? Would alumni and potential benefactors be scandalized? Would students from mainland China stop registering at M.I.T.? Would professors at Stanford curb their research? Would urban comprehensive universities not secure the blessings of liberty?

OTHER VOICES, OTHER VIEWS

From the President of a Public University:

The pace of life of a college president is something one can never believe unless one experiences it. Frequently, days involve breakfast, lunch, and dinner meetings, sessions after dinner, and then coming home to face the mail, the reading, and the correspondence. This is the norm. I don't know if one could say the hours are 65 or 70 per week, but the truth is that the job is seven days a week, morning, noon and night. You are always on call.

In addition, one needs to shift gears continually. A fifteen-minute crisis is followed by a lecture to the faculty on budget which must be very calm and reassuring. This is followed by a hectic call from a trustee, which is followed by a lunch with area businessmen. You must enter into each session well prepared, calm, cool, and collected and make it appear as if that particular hour of the day is the most important to you. The frantic pace is one of the most difficult things about a presidency, and it is one of the big differences from any other job on campus. It is not the same when you are the vice-president or director. It takes a toll on your family life, your social life, and whatever else you can do.

I have only found time to visit the dry cleaner once in six months; I have to ask my spouse or someone else to do that. I find it very difficult to get to the dentist (I delayed an appointment for four months). These kinds of things should not be, but I am afraid they are the norm because there is always something more pressing to do than to attend to personal things that are also very important.

From the Provost and Dean of a Public University:

I've often felt guilty (albeit briefly) because I don't seem to work as long or as hard as others say they do. I think it's because I forget to count the many breakfasts, dinners, and evening events as work and because I virtually never take home work. I learned a long time ago that it's not how long or how hard you work, it's whether you get the job done successfully that counts. I do, and do it quickly.

I work at a hyperkinetic pace, but in waves. My assistant shows me no scheduling mercy, and when I say I want 25 appointments, she schedules them for me that week. She has the bad habit also of believing me when I say I want to turn around letters in 48 hours. Actually, it's really she who leads a hyperkinetic worklife, come to think of it.

From the Acting President of a Public College:

An administrator, particularly a president, will lead a busy life. The administrator has only him- or herself to blame if it is hyperkinetic. In general there will be a team of vice-presidents and deans with whom the task of representing the college may be shared.

One does need to be very clear about priorities and how an appearance, or lack thereof, will further or hinder the attainment of institutional goals. *No* is a useful word and its use should be mastered.

Heavy family responsibilities are generally not compatible with the schedule college presidents normally follow.

From the Vice-President for Academic Affairs at a Public University:

As I dictate a rough outline for this item, I am riding in my car on the way to work. I have been up since 5:00 a.m. reading mail and doing memos so that I can handle the back-to-back meeting schedule for today. Of course, the half-hour set aside for lunch will be chewed up by a meeting that runs a bit too long, some phone calls that must be made, the electronic mail that must be answered, and the faculty member who absolutely has to have one minute of my time. This will go on until about 6:00 p.m. when I leap in the car to rush home so that I can be late for dinner.

Meanwhile nagging at the back of my mind are the major projects I have to move ahead: the analysis of indicators of teaching quality the president wants me to write; the national data study I'm doing with a colleague; and the fact that the bathroom needs wallpapering.

Do I consider this hyperkinetic? I suppose so, but I don't consider it unusual. It's been going this way for years and I see no forces at hand to change it.

If I were to appoint another assistant, it would probably simply add to my workload because we would pick up all of those things we haven't attended to over the past few years. I'm not sure how many of those are important enough to justify a new person, but I suspect I would be a better vice-president if I got them done. And so it goes, day in and day out. Am I complaining? Not at all. I'm simply describing what I believe is the normal life of any senior administrator.

No one forces me to do this and if I didn't like it I would just walk away.

I suspect that the bank vice-president, the insurance company regional manager, or the computer company vice-president for marketing have equally frantic lives. Perhaps their employees demand a bit less of their time, but face-to-face discussion is a reality of higher education. From my intermittent observations my perception is that senior officials in any large organization who are dedicated to improving the organization work long and demanding hours. I can only assume that the intrinsic rewards of accomplishment, self-esteem, and reaching organizational goals are the rewards that people seek in these jobs. It certainly isn't appreciation by employees or clientele; the administrator is the perpetual outsider and heretic.

Therefore, I have to conclude that if administrators have hyperkinetic workstyles it is a result of choices they have made in exchange for rewards that they value.

From the Dean of a Public College:

For the conscientious administrator in a leanly staffed institution, this is not a myth but a reality. There are, however, variables: personal conscientiousness and adequacy of staffing in one's area vis-a-vis the amount of work that has to be done.

In casual conversations with colleagues, I find that the vast majority at least *report feeling* harried.

From the President of a Private College:

It depends on:

1. The geographic scatter of important constituencies, and particularly of sources of funding.

2. Travel budgets, for example, the availability of "perks" such as a driver or permission to travel first class that make constantly being in motion tolerable.

3. Self discipline. Read: H. A. Simon on Gresham's law of organizational behavior where he shows that routine

trivia tend to drive out planning; Drucker or Peters on the importance of focus and selectivity in the use of time.

4. Competence of staff—at solving problems that should not wind up on your desk, and in keeping you away from things you should trust them to handle.

You are never likely to feel you've earned the title, "Your Serene Highness," and with sports, social events, and student life, it is hard to keep your schedule from being a seven-day one, year-round; but whether or not you become the campus ping-pong ball remains your choice. The grizzled plant manager's boast that "I don't get ulcers; I give 'em" is a bit brutal—but it is a reminder that your life and your time, despite the occasional emergency, are yours to try to manage and control.

From the Dean of Arts and Sciences at a Public College:

When I compare my life as an administrator to life as a faculty member, I notice a significant difference in the nature of my involvement in projects. As a faculty member, I conceived, developed, and executed a limited number of projects (a research paper, a new course proposal, etc.) in a given time span. As an administrator, I participate in a large number of projects, but my participation in each is limited. The total amount of time spent in "work" is probably about the same, but the fragmentation of administrative work leads me to perceive my work life as hyperkinetic.

Another factor leading to a perception of an administrator's life as hyperkinetic is the fact that so much of our time is consumed in responding to the initiatives of others.

From the Dean of a College of Arts and Sciences at a Public University:

The kinds of issues that confront administrators, and the pace with which those issues present themselves, favor selection of *relatively* hyperkinetic people from the faculty ranks. I've met very few academic administrators who believe that their primary job is to manage the status quo, or who believe that they can afford to approach the major challenges of their institutions at leisure. I think that most of us have a large backlog of issues that we are trying to find time to address. In such circumstances, the real trick is to meld a necessarily hyperkinetic career with an equally necessary peace in the rest of one's life.

From the Chancellor of a Public University:

During the first months of any administrative job, people simply want to see you, probe your position on issues, and discover whether you are human or not. I have found the first few months of any new position frenetic if not hyperkinetic. After that, I feel, you can control to a larger degree the schedule and provide a better pace for the day, week, and month. Certain times of the year call for an excessively busy schedule, but that is to be expected. So while there is truth to the statement [myth], it should not be exaggerated. These are demanding positions and they take energy and enthusiasm. I do not think that an administrator must live a hyperkinetic life.

From the Assistant to the Vice-President for Academic Affairs at a Public University:

Most administrators do lead hyperkinetic lives, but for most of them it isn't necessary. The image of administrators is that they are always "swamped" and so most of us arrange to be swamped. If we aren't actually heavily burdened, we say we are, lest we fail to exhibit the macho image we are expected to project, and that we need psychologically in order to keep up with the administrative Joneses.

Decades of administrators building that kind of image and accompanying work style create the expectation that we will show up everywhere for everything. The imagery of being present at all sorts of events and meeting with every individual and group that feels entitled to access to the person at the top has become very important to success. A good deal of hyperkinesis is simply being places.

If, perchance, there is a slack period, we feel guilty about relaxing. Since there is always something new that might be done, we tend to use the down time to generate new activities, which means that when the time for implementation and follow-up comes at a busy period we are more harried than ever.

Administrators like to be involved in things, so when an invitation comes to participate in a new and interesting activity, we find it hard to say no.

From the Provost of a Public University:

The more energetic and driven one's superior, the more diffused and therefore hyperkinetic one's own life.

From the Provost of a Public University:

It is true that academic administration makes a fine career for a person with a short attention span. If she is bored with anything she is doing at any time of the day, she need only wait half an hour or so and the subjects will be changed: Another meeting and possibly another meeting!

But hyperkinesis is the lazy administrator's way out. Robert Hutchins took ten years to reverse his field on the proposition, which he had advanced in an earlier article, that impatience is a necessary characteristic for the administrator. Ten years later he decided that patience was a greater virtue than impatience.

I would rather argue that the successful administrator's life is a constant battle against the lure of hyperkinesis. It is all too easy to give every problem a lick and a promise, and to eschew the painfully slow work of analysis on which the resolution of difficult problems depends. Administrators spend most of their time touching bases, and this is an essential part of their work, but there is no value to carrying all your constituencies with you in the wrong direction.

From the Dean of a College of Liberal Arts at a Public University:

One's own personality and stamina dictate to some extent the degree of freneticism one can sustain, but the personality and stamina of peers and superiors also influence each individual's attempts to live or to resist the frenetic life.

Sustained freneticism tends to focus on the visible at the expense of the necessary, to focus on deadlines at the expense of overview, to focus on the "quick fix" at the expense of the thoughtful. Ideally, one finds ways to do the necessary rather than the visible.

From the Vice-President for Academic Affairs at a Public College:

With rare exception, academic administrators I have known at the level of dean or above lead hyperkinetic lives. The ambiguities of academic leadership plus the "flatness" of academic organization require deep involvement by such administrators. Demands by state agencies on public institutions and national organizations on all institutions add extensive travel to an already busy schedule. For administrators the watchword may well be "commute or perish."

From the Vice-President for Academic Affairs at a Public University:

It's evidence enough that I have taken so long to respond to this request that I now worry that it's too late. My first year was supposed to be a lot of "listening and learning," but I arrived to a list of 14 items that the president wanted me to address as soon as possible—including such major items as criteria for sabbaticals and the registration system. I was also to address a major crisis in athletics in my first six weeks.

It has never stopped. So many issues and problems come across my desk that even a super type A personality like myself has to prioritize, to make choices which leave serious problems untouched. I do *hard work* 60+ hours a week which does not include all the concerts, athletic events, and dinners I am supposed to attend.

In my experience, this is *not* a myth. Do I like it—and my job? I would if more of the time were devoted to goals I thought important and I had more support for what I was doing. Then it might not seem or be so hyper.

From the Vice-President for Academic Affairs at a Public University:

If any of the administrators who respond find truth in this myth, they should undertake a restrospective review of their goals and reevaluate their priorities.

Chapter 3

An Administrator Will Inherit Untouchables

A portion of the excitement generated by a letter of appointment to an administrative post is inspired by hope. All the lessons that have been mastered and the experience that has been saved can be carefully tied to the car-top carrier and brought to the new campus; all the unwise decisions, precipitous acts, and sins of commission and omission unworthy of the administrator one strives to be can be discarded in the dustbins behind Old Main on the campus of one's younger self. One will surely score more spectacular runs in another ballpark.

The hope is not so naive as a description of it might suggest, for one is not born an academic administrator, and even those with considerable leadership talent must spend years perfecting it. Additionally, the sophisticated understand that an administrator neither leads nor manages out of context. The dimensions and condition of the ballpark do matter; the abilities and dedication of fellow players do affect outcomes. Many a director of admissions has made a president appear prescient and many a dean has contributed to the failure of a provost. Hence, whether, when, and how to effect personnel changes are questions to wear down many a senior administrator's worry beads.

One need not have spent many years in academic administration to have met one or more incompetent or indolent "survivors." Every campus harbors its unfortunate share of administrators, both line and staff, who inspire wonder in those who come to learn the degree to which they approach ineptness and/or inertia without apparent consequences. Some will even boast of having survived a certain number of presidents, deans, or directors. In social settings the more radical fringe have been known to entertain a group by recounting the methods recommended for eliminating over-enthusiastic, over-energetic senior administrators.

There are perhaps as many profiles of these survivors as there are survivors: some, in accord with the Peter Principle, have been promoted beyond their abilities; some, for causes that grow outside the university's boundaries, are aggrieved or depressed; some, for a host of complex reasons, are contemporary Bartlebys "who prefer not to." The characteristics and talents of the survivors will differ widely; their mode of operation, however, will often be so similar that one begins to suspect the existence of an underground manual: *Ten Easy Steps to Sabotaging Excellence,* or its companion volume, *In Pursuit of the Ineffectual Manager.* Indeed, this common mode of operation serves in many ways as protective covering against the onslaught of those who might have the temerity to attempt any change in any domain.

These survivors have become "untouchables" in the minds of some for two chief reasons linked to this widespread mode of operation: First, the survivors, nearly without exception, have assumed the manners of the good soul. Yes, indeed, they would be delighted to work on this or that project; they have just been waiting for the opportunity finally to get this or that office in order; they have for years been proposing the very plans that are at last being coordinated. If your predecessor had had your foresight, the university would not now be struggling with this or that difficulty. They bow, they smile, they bring good cheer; they regale a new administrator with stories of past campus happenings; they impress many, including themselves, with the purity of their intentions and their devotion to State U.; and, above all, they gossip. They will confide their concerns about your leadership sotto voce in corridors and dining rooms; they will, with furrowed brow, reluctantly reveal the method you purportedly plan to use to tarnish the institution's seal.

Second, long before the notion of "support group" had been popularized, survivors in the academy had developed an appreciation of its advantages and had mastered the techniques of establishing coalitions, not so much of the like-minded as of the variably disaffected or ambitious. And the strength of these coalitions is not dismissed with impunity, for they frequently include members of the outside community who are at times exceedingly naive in interpreting the academic script they have been given to read.

Thus, by means of bonhomie, the survivors inspire sympathy, for we all fear meeting challenges we cannot meet; and, by means of alliances, they inspire caution, for we have all witnessed the irrationality of crowd behavior.

To inherit a survivor, however, as newly appointed administrators assuredly will, is not to inherit an untouchable unless one is paralyzed by sympathy or caution as one's predecessor presumably was when writing out a will containing unwelcome bequests. With this understanding, certain guiding principles should apply when formulating answers to whether, when, and how one should attempt to bring about the transfiguration of a survivor.

Whether One Should

A university campus, with its honored tradition of academic freedom and with its cherished, slightly anarchical management habits, constitutes a totally inappropriate backdrop for the staging of a purification crusade. Hence, an administrator's purpose in dismissing a survivor or in changing a survivor's responsibilities should not be to cleanse the land or to reawaken the community to the glories of the work ethic. And to draw attention to an administrator's purpose is crucial, for no decision maker ever succeeds in completely disguising either the overt or covert reasons for any act in a setting where hundreds of trained interpreters of tone and voice think their thoughts.

Consequently, the answer to whether one should seek the resignation or the transfer of a survivor must attach itself not to the reform of an individual, an unlikely happening, but to the aspirations of an institution and to the responsibilities that have been assigned to a college, department, or division as part of a concerted effort to reach specified heights. Any university survivor, from any office or division, who cannot or will not meet fair and just expectations is metamorphosed into an untouchable at the expense of students. Only in the rarest of circumstances, if ever, should the category untouchable be recognized as serving the long-term greater good of a university.

When One Should

Even if one agrees that survivors are counterfeit untouchables and that an administrator who has inherited one or more must transcend both false compassion and unbecoming fear in dealing with them, the question of timing remains. How soon after full recognition and understanding of the problem should one move to address it? And, just as important, how long should it take a senior administrator to reach conclusions regarding the effectiveness of those who report to him or her?

While avoiding a foolish specificity, while accepting slight variations in cultural climate from campus to campus, and while admitting varied degrees of complexity due to size and governing structures, experienced administrators should most certainly have an accurate survey of the newly acquired land in their minds if not in their files in a matter of a few months. Prudence and related virtues to the contrary, administrators who leave one campus for another are not immigrating to a foreign country and should not think themselves rash in advocating certain changes in a very short period of time. American colleges and universities publish 3,200 different mission statements, hire marketing teams to promote distinguishable identities, and pay artists to create individualized logos. However, the variations in language, ideals, values, manners, and mores from one campus to another are often so slight as to be discerned by no one but the initiated—and the initiated are able to master them very quickly. Indeed, any university that has invited consultants to its shores has admitted that visitors from other parts of the academic world are not from foreign lands since they are trusted to proffer advice on everything from the quality of degree programs to the methods of recruiting students to the strategies of fund raising after having often spent only a few days on campus. Accreditation teams would become paralyzed were they to begin their site visits by questioning the premise of a common language and common basic values for all colleges and universities. Every national conference also accepts as one of its postulates a language and mores common to academicians across the country. Furthermore, the more vivid differences occur, when at all, between the public and private institutions and between community colleges and liberal arts colleges and universities, and research has shown that administrators tend to move within these categories as opposed to moving from one to another. Consequently, an administrator with a trained eye will spot survivors at some distance, will list all the characteristics that have marked them as untouchables, and, recognizing that nothing can be gained by delay, will act within months of his or her arrival to affect a change.

How One Should

An administrator will inherit, along with one or more survivors, a number of conditions that will influence and complicate the decisions to be made about them. For example, administrators who manage large units in large universities often have more options when making decisions than do administrators who head small departments in small colleges. Size alone will nearly always increase flexibility. The president of even a medium-size university, inheriting an incompetent assistant who has already survived two presidents, might easily find him or her a position somewhere on campus that is in keeping with the assistant's skills. However, to dismiss or not to dismiss may be the only options for the president of a small liberal arts college. The director of admissions who evaluates the performance of twenty admission counselors might well conclude that a veteran of fifteen years who exaggerates his or her recruiting efforts on the road might perform with integrity under close supervision in the home office. On the contrary, the director of admissions who with two colleagues must attract three hundred freshmen to a small college in an isolated town in the Northeast does not have the luxury of multiple choices when one of the two assistants cannot or will not carry a fair share of the assigned responsibilities.

Whether to dismiss, demote, or transfer a survivor; whether to move out, down, or sideways; whether to reconfigure a given set of responsibilities are decisions that conditions other than size will propel or constrain. Indeed, size merely provides flexibility; it does not prescribe using flexibility for the sake of ease. An administrator soon learns that these conditions are not only exceedingly large in number, but that the variations upon their themes are nearly infinite. Hence, guideposts can only point to principles that should obtain in decision making in these matters.

Sartre and other philosophers have claimed that man cannot lie to himself. If so, except in cases of pathological delusion, a survivor has not only assessed his or her performance with a fair degree of accuracy, but on some level has admitted that an excessive amount of time is spent in ineffectual attempts to convince others of his or her value. Few relish a life dominated by the fear of being found out, and a number of survivors welcome the opportunity to start afresh when allowed to do so with dignity. Many view with some bitterness, even with contempt, administrators who have participated in their "cover up." Hence, the place for an administrator to begin is with the survivor and not with those who will react to the change that is being contemplated.

One president remembers that as a child, he enjoyed weekly radio programs that he and his father gave themselves as "treats" at the end of a day's labor. He admits that one did not tune in to the "Fibber Magee and Molly" show for moments of epiphany. However, insight often comes from unexpected sources, and at the age of eight or nine, he found one of these shows to be a source of light that time never extinguished. Fibber Magee and his fellow townspeople decided to organize a parade to honor the "common man." The plot of the show consisted of efforts to find a person in town who would represent the common man at the head of the proposed parade. The drums never banged and the citizens never marched because no one would accept the honor. Every person in town thought of himself as uncommon, distinctive in some way.

Survivors are not exempt from this human need to believe that their contributions to an institution's advancement are both distinctive and meaningful. The trouble comes when, for whatever reason, they lose confidence and begin to rationalize in order to continue thinking well of themselves: the demands made upon them are inordinate, or their talents are unrecognized, or their supervisors are nonsupportive.

Indeed, this universal need for distinction often manifests itself among the survivors who are not engaged in passive resistance in what one might call the "switch phenomenon." In such cases, a person who cannot or will not perform assigned responsibilities will enthusiastically assume others of his or her own choosing and will respond with anger and bitterness if rewards do not follow. An example is an assistant to the president whose primary obligation centers on government relations. For any of a dozen possible reasons, this assistant becomes bored with government reports and with walking the halls of the legislature. She decides that what the president needs is not better information on upcoming legislative bills but better institutional data. At first,

the reformatting of student profiles into more useful spread-
sheets is simply an addition to her primary responsibilities.
In time however, this work that she enjoys leads to her ne-
glecting that which has ceased to interest her.

If this assistant is given a mediocre performance rating,
she is likely to feel and to express outrage. She will refer to
her hard work, her imaginative response to a real need, and
her unappreciated and unrewarded devotion. To have allowed this person to map her own route is to have unwit-
tingly contributed to the making of a malcontent. In Peter
Shaffer's play, *Lettice and Lovage*, the central character
serves as a humorous exemplar of such behavioral response.
An eccentric, middle-aged English woman works as a docent
in a country estate that has become a historical monument.
She has grown bored beyond endurance by her own telling
and retelling of the stories associated with the house to one
group of gawking tourists after another. So she begins to invent dramatic tales whose plots and characters she substitutes for the historically accurate ones. Confronted by a supervisor, who seeks to know the provenance of these
arresting tales, the docent vehemently accuses the supervisor of harboring an unromantic soul in an age that encourages pedestrian minds. Administrators such as the president's assistant under discussion are valiant in their efforts
to convince themselves and others that supervisors and universities and even the times seek the common when an elevated sight would allow them a view of the distinctive.

In this and similar survival cases, the president must
decide whether the real need is for another institutional researcher or for a government relations officer. Administrators simply must not be allowed to invent their own job descriptions according to the changing needs of their psyches
without regard to the real needs and priorities of the institution—any more than docents should be permitted to ward
off boredom by fabricating stories for their own entertainment. In addition, if the president avoids confronting this
assistant, he or she will keep one more administrator who
rationalizes stratagems of survival instead of leading an authentic professional life.

No university can afford personnel whose energies are directed toward persuading themselves and others that they are not "common men" or who attack those they suspect of characterizing them as such. Hence, if a survivor can be re-inspired to perform his or her present job, fine. If, in less rare instances, moving a survivor laterally will help both the university and the individual, excellent. But if a survivor must be moved down or discharged, one should not hesitate to act, for euphemism of behavior is ultimately no more kind than euphemism of language is honest.

In conference with the employee, the administrator, kindly but firmly, should outline expectations that have not been met and explore options for the purpose of reaching an agreement. At times, such meetings will conclude with the mapping of a viable route within or without the institution for those who have been assigned responsibilities that are, for whatever complex reasons, beyond their reach. However, there are cases in which self-esteem is inextricably bound to a title, or self-assessment is delusional, or self-protection is the response of choice to authority. For these, no conference, however skillfully and considerately structured, is likely to succeed. At these times, an administrator must guard against slipping into inertia, for under such atmospheric conditions, the experienced can forecast the severity of storms and know that they must take the time to check the strength of the sea walls and to shore up any section that might appear to be weak.

With constituents internal to the campus, this checking and shoring up will include consulting with appropriate fellow administrators or faculty to determine the position of any survivor's division or office in relation to commonly envisioned and attainable goals. The tone of such consultative decision making should be as far removed from vindictiveness or pettiness as possible. With constituents external to the campus, the challenge is to balance a sincere respect for their views with an equally sincere desire to remain uninfluenced by purely political considerations.

Just as faculty in their teaching and research must never renounce or withhold truth to meet any community's ephemeral needs, an administrator must never sacrifice a right decision to receive any community's temporary approval. Only the naive will judge such advice to be naive. To avoid conflict at the cost of integrity even once is to signal a pattern of behavior that the unscrupulous or the ambitious will immediately depend upon and they will become doubly irate should their expectations not be met in the future. Idealism is not naivety. A university's mission is to promote the first and to dispel the second. For a university to fulfill its mission, its administrators must understand the distinction between the two.

Prudence, like meekness, is a virtue complex enough to study in some depth, but not glamorous enough to attract, let alone to keep, our attention. No one stands at the stage door to witness its comings and goings. Hence, in many instances we are not certain what lies beneath the stage makeup. When, for example, does prudence mask faintheartedness? Our reluctance to seek an answer to that difficult question may be linked to our lack of enthusiasm for photo opportunities when in the company of prudence. We want to be seen embracing honesty and shaking hands with courage, but we do not like to be caught holding hands with prudence. Indeed, to be praised as "prudent" is to wonder whether one has been praised at all. The virtue carries a cachet that is slightly bourgeois, slightly Right Bank.

And yet, we have all witnessed administrators delay personnel decisions, at times indefinitely, in the name of prudence: fund raisers who raise nothing but concern, heads of advancement divisions who do not understand the nature of universities, assistants who spread confusion by means of illiterate memos. All have been known to grow old without the slightest interruption to their days and ways. They have become, so the myth goes, untouchables. They have played second violin so long that one excuses the glazed look and the uninspired adagios, or they have too many friends on the board of directors to require that they stay awake during rehearsals.

Nonsense. Longevity should not be given more than its due, and even brothers-in-law of members of the state legislature, neighbors of the commissioner of education, and friends of the president of the alumni association should bear the consequences of fair and honest performance evaluations. In nearly every case, the harm done an institution by years of neglect or incompetence in one of its parts far outweighs the harm done to it by the hostilities, most often temporary, rising from a legitimate and wisely handled personnel change.

Ironically, those who do not make these demanded changes often seem not to decide against making them, but seem rather to postpone making them or to avoid thinking about the advisability of making them. And therein lies part of the danger. For no college or university can afford senior administrators who slip into what Lionel Trilling, in another context, has called "the morality of inertia"—a morality that makes decisions by not making decisions.

OTHER VOICES, OTHER VIEWS

From the President of a Private College:

The only untouchables, as one university president apparently found out recently to his chagrin and demise, are the knees of female staff members.

Otherwise, a president will likely find a mix—some "recommended untouchables" and some "self-assumed untouchables." The trick with the former is to sort out the quality of the recommendations, separating recommendations based on merit from those based on politics—and remembering that the most vital to preserve may include those of a secretary or a custodian as much as those of a tenured chairholder on the faculty. The challenge with the latter is to assess the merit, the political power, and the degrees of self-delusion involved and to move quickly to establish that you intend discussions of activities and performance to be a two-way street. Egregious bluffs that the campus will be watching should be called early, and even more complicated, sensitive negotiations ought to still get an early start, even if the explorations and the resolutions take time.

Even though we now frown on most of it for freshmen, hazing remains a part of all entries into new systems. Presidents, especially those who will believe in fraternities and sororities, should expect a bit of it; and they will get no protection from the anti-hazing statutes.

From the President of a Public University

This is not a myth but a truism. Untouchables include personnel, programs, and "ways of doing business." Some can be nudged over time in one direction or another and perhaps ultimately dealt with on their merits, but, at the point of inheritance, a prudent administrator will make his or her impact by fighting battles he or she has a better chance of winning.

From the President of a Public University:

There may be, for some administrators, persons inherited who cannot, under any circumstances, at any time, be "touched," that is, fired or otherwise disempowered. I have not encountered, to my knowledge, any people who had that degree of untouchability. And that is the point, I suppose: untouchability is more likely a matter of degree. Touching may lead to badly burned fingers, of course. Thus an administrator may (or will) inherit people who should be marked "Flammable—Handle With Care." But they are still touchable; one should simply be prepared for some pain in laying hands on them. The pain presumably varies with the flammability and the amount of care taken in the handling. Risks have to be calculated.

I have heard numerous stories of untouchables in other institutions: the vice-president who has been there a ton of years and has many friends on the governing board and on other seats of power; or the football coach who operates outside the institution's normal process of governance; or the dean who has built a base of power among external constituents served by his college; or even the middle manager who over the years has aggregated unto himself authority well

beyond that required of his position. I cannot say how true
these stories are, though they have been related to me on
occasion by presidents who tried to touch such people and
suffered consequences more dire than singed fingers.

I have known people at my own institution in my years
(11) as president who answered more or less to these descriptions. Only one could be said to have been untouchable. The
others I found I could deal with, though not always easily.

As to the one who could not be dealt with, well, he was
a dean of long standing. He had an entrenched (and apparently deserved) reputation of being able to get presidents
fired if they crossed him. He had protection, and he was
powerful. The emphasis here should be on "was." He is not
the dean any more. What can happen with untouchability is
change. Circumstances change, protection and power wane
(or may wax, I suppose). That is what happened with my
dean. There was a bit of change, a bit of waning, a bit of
reckless behavior. I fired him. It was a struggle, but I made
it stick and survived. So, in the end (though not at the beginning) he was a touchable.

I guess I would conclude that this myth carries with it
a kernel of wisdom, a grain of truth. Baldly stated, it may be
more the exception than the rule. But, given a little leaven-
ing, some elaboration, it cannot, I think, be dismissed out of
hand.

This myth is, I grant you, among the "clichés of the
academy," as you put it. Still, clichés get to be that way because they have, or had, some basis in truth.

From the Acting President of a Public College:

A good administrator will not inherit untouchables. He or
she might inherit persons or issues which take a bit more
time and skill to address, but to admit something is untouchable is to admit defeat. The advent of a new administrator
is one of the few opportunities to turn things upside down. In
many cases, it is expected and desired. The ability to bring a
new perspective to a problem and the opportunity to establish a new vision for the institution allows changes which
would be unthinkable at other times.

Clearly, there will be some tough nuts to crack. A great deal of time may have to be invested by a new administrator in building a constituency and consensus prior to moving on an entrenched person, policy, or procedure, but inability to do so will severely undermine a new administrator.

Untouchables should be read "opportunities" by a good administrator.

From the President of a Private College:

I was once part of an institution with an enrollment of 400 and a faculty of 30 and *two* deans—one of whom was a hold-over from a past administration. Every college has its share of holdovers or untouchables. How nice to have been living in an earlier day when it was expected that when the boss left, the staff submitted resignations, and the new boss was free to pick and choose among them. No longer the case, but nonetheless eventually a president must create his own staff, regardless of holdovers.

Then, as for faculty, how many untouchables are kept in place by the tenure system?

From the Acting Dean of a College at a Public University:

If one takes a narrow view of "untouchables," then my guess is that such individuals are relatively few in number. I refer to individuals who are politically well connected and are protected both by the system and their connections. Further, I would argue that only a small sub-class of such individuals would be regarded as untouchables, namely, the sub-class that is performing unsatisfactorily, for that is the only context for which the issue of untouchables would arise.

On the other hand, it is probably true that all administrators would like to make changes among their faculty and staff. They may experience frustration from the realization that the built-in protection within the system makes change involving personnel very difficult. In this sense, we all have numbers of protected faculty who are effectively "untouchables." I have addressed this question in terms of personnel, but I believe a parallel situation exists regarding programs.

From the Vice-President of a Private College:

It is probably the case that the mythology of every campus assumes that certain people, programs, and/or practices are untouchables. To a large extent, the new administrator's success in dealing with those untouchables has to do with his or her political skills, charisma, patience, etc. But it is also possible that the degree to which he or she is committed to change will have something to do with the ultimate outcome. Perhaps that old song about the ram that kept butting the dam "cuz he had high hopes" is relevant—at least some of the time. Of course, it is also possible that the ram will be washed downstream and off the scene when he persists to the point of breaking through the resistance provided by whoever or whatever is interested in maintaining the dam.

From the Dean of Arts and Sciences at a Private University:

University "problems" which won't go away are passed along the line and inevitably end up in the new administrator's office. The hope—maybe expectation—is that some creative thought from a new administrator will "answer the problem." We all do it, but in truth it seems that everything has been tried and problems continue to be passed around until they exit the loop for one reason or another.

From the Vice-President for Academic Affairs at a Private University:

There are tenured professors and professors nearing retirement who are somewhat untouchable in the sense that it's not worth the trouble it would cause to get them to change their ways. "They've always been chair of those departments; to remove them would show disrespect for their long years of service to the institution." Or, "His gruff attitude toward students may alienate a few of them, but he'll be retiring next year, so let's not make waves." There are programs, schedules, calendars that "have always been done that way" and change would upset too many people.

On the other hand, an "untouchable" will become "touched" real fast if it becomes obvious that it is causing the institution to lose money.

From the Vice-President for Academic Affairs at a Public University:

More often than not the administrator does inherit untouchables. This is unfortunate since some untouchables have more power and assume more authority than even the president or a higher administrator in the organization

From the Provost of a Public University:

Take the time to learn the culture of the campus; learn where the skeletons are buried. Stick by your convictions and do what is right. There are no untouchables.

From the Chancellor of a Public University:

Why do you call it a "myth"?

Chapter 4

An Administrator Will Yearn for the Classroom

Having driven over a day with an unusual number of pot-holes, an academic administrator may recall, with some nostalgia, his or her former serene self carrying a green Harvard book bag across a quiet quad. However, even a superficial probing will reveal that the temporary mourning of things past is for youth and its infinite possibilities rather than for the paths not taken. For the truth is that most mid-level and senior administrators who wished to become non-administrators could effect the transformation. Studies show that the provenance of the majority of academic deans, vice-presidents, and presidents is the land of the faculty and many still hold valid passports. They are not expounding on the cantos of the Inferno or on William James' pragmatism in Room 36 of West Hall on Monday, Wednesday, and Friday for one simple reason: they prefer management to teaching.

This reason, stripped of euphemisms and boldly stated, continues to summon its little *frisson*, its small shock among the intelligentsia. Thus non-diplomatically hurled, it also continues to elicit faint disdain among the faculty who worry that, in this case, truth-telling may come dangerously close to vulgarity.

Therefore, administrators, well versed in and sympathetic to the culture of the academy, perpetuate variations on a myth that would have them returning to the classroom if only they could. One did not really seek to be a dean, but agreed to bear this cross for the sake of his or her beloved college after the search committee could not agree on the merits of outside candidates. Another wishes that the cup of the vice-presidency had not been offered, but will drink it to the dregs since he or she made the mistake of lifting it to lips that were reluctant to begin with. A third, after fifteen years in administrative posts, still misses the classroom and envies those whose assigned responsibilities are there. Yet a fourth had decided to return to teaching after his or her children had obtained their degrees, but five years after the deadline is still completing certain projects before leaving office.

Both the rationalizing and the rhetoric that attempts to disguise it are touching for two reasons. One, the tone and the substance of the explanations concede that the core of an academic institution is its classrooms, its library, and its laboratories—not its administrative offices and meeting rooms. Two, the accounting and the language that buffers it bow to an academic culture that unhappily fosters a need to apologize in far too many of its administrators whose talents and dedication are essential to the growth and quality of any college or university.

Even graduate students pursuing degrees in higher education often formulate questionnaires the tone of which suggests that an administrator of your intelligence might have responded to a higher calling. Just beneath the surface of the questions rumbles a gee whiz, gosh, by golly wonderment as to why you chose to become the president of a university when you might have collated the manuscript variants of medieval homilies. Indeed, a recent questionnaire, reflecting the researcher's attempt to understand why someone would accept a senior-level administrative position in a university, asked the respondent to check something resembling one of the following: (a)Prestige, (b) Money, (c) Enjoyment of the work—and, then, as if winded after this run of the imagination, simply added (d) Other. Perhaps you are engaged in the ritual killing off of your parents. Did they ever get beyond high school? Maybe you are the product of an authoritarian church and you savor the last word. Do you think of those who work with you as subordinates? It may well be that you are compensating for the lack of a satisfying human relationship. How long have you been divorced?

In sum, in the academy, when discussing those who profess and those who administer, two unquestioned premises often obtain. Those who chose to devote their professional lives to teaching and research did so for motives that transcend the self. Those who decided to spend their careers engaged in management, broadly defined so as to include leadership, did so for reasons that center on the self. Hence, one is able to trust the first group, but must be wary of the second.

However, administrators who signal their eagerness to return to the classroom at the first opportunity not only sense the endemic mistrust of those who left it for whatever reason in the first place, but also understand other cultural phenomena that make of all campuses one world that at times struggles to tolerate those who would govern it.

To begin with, a college or university is as class conscious as a British social club. Its crest and seal are what really matter, not its logos and marketing slogans. Hierarchical thinking reigns without apology, and intellectual meritocracy orders the ranking of everything from graduate schools to profiles of entering freshmen. The class system places the Ivy Leaguers in the aristocratic box seats, the community colleges in the second balcony, and all others here and there in the orchestra and mezzanine. But even the location of the box seats and the "here and there" in the rest of the hall are a matter of concern to position-conscious academics.

Edward Shils, professor of sociology and social thought at the University of Chicago, in a perceptive, fifty-year-backward glance at the university world, tells us that this passion for distinguishing the aristocracy from the haute bourgeoisie from the petite bourgeoisie is a fairly recent phenomenon—

one that, quite ironically, has grown in the same household as the passion against what is perceived to be elitism. In recalling his student days at the University of Pennsylvania, he writes: "We never thought about Harvard or Columbia or Princeton. Nor did we feel inferior to them. . . . Each university was sui generis" (*American Scholar*, Spring, 1982, pp. 164–65). In referring to his early days as an instructor at the University of Chicago, which was somewhat more self-conscious than others about its place in the sun, he nevertheless points out: "There was a vague sense of the hierarchy of universities, but it was not acutely felt. A person who had a doctorate from Chicago did not think that he was exiled from the Elysian Fields if he took a post at Vanderbilt or Utah. The hypersensitivity to rank, which is characteristic of the 'anti-elitist' decades in which we are now living, had not yet appeared. . . . Fifty years ago it was not regarded as a mortification to be appointed to a university located somewhere else than 'where the action is,' to use another of the phrases of the egalitarian anti-elitists" (Shils, pp. 166–67).

Academics do not limit their class consciousness to an ordering of institutions within the broad slots of the Carnegie taxonomy of colleges and universities, but extend their nets far enough to catch all the disciplines. Mathematicians sneer at the work done by recreational therapists; epidemiologists refuse offices in the school of nursing; industrial engineers speak patronizingly about the research of industrial technologists; and philosophers question the propriety of giving academic rank to ballet masters.

But the fat lady has only begun to sing. While the professor of English has inherited a more prestigious title than the professor of communication arts, there are sub-divisions of class within the field of English. Anyone who has ever walked across a campus knows that to theorize about anything at all is more elevated an activity than to apply anything at all. The question of worth is to be or not to be, not to do or not to do. Hence, critical theorists get a better seat than teachers of writing for business and industry. Furthermore, your seriousness as a scholar is tied in part to the distance you place between yourself and the contemporary. The study of Old English strong verbs outranks the study of the rhetorical devices in the plays of Tennessee Williams.

The variations on this theme are nearly endless. However, the point to be made is that ignorance or denial of the hierarchical mind-set of the university culture weakens an academic administrator in at least two ways. Decisions made without consideration of this context may well lead to projects that are doomed to failure. Witness the attempt some years back at the University of Toronto and elsewhere to mount an M.Phil. degree as a substitute for a Ph.D. for students primarily interested in teaching. Virtually no one willingly made room for a degree that was immediately branded as less prestigious than the Ph.D., and those misguided enough to enroll in an M.Phil. program became object lessons of academic class consciousness.

Furthermore, an administrator who does not understand the hierarchical thinking that characterizes the campus culture is in danger of responding emotionally and inappropriately when he or she is reminded, at times subtly and at times rudely, of his or her rank in the academic procession. Every scholar understands that someone has to raise money, court legislators, please alumni, and balance budgets, but few will allow themselves to be distracted by such peripheral activities if they seem to be handled reasonably well, and even fewer will feel anything resembling gratitude for a senior administrator's seventy-hour weeks dedicated to such mundane pursuits. In the academy, what counts is not what one does, but what one knows; and knowing something about institutional strategic planning and generic models for deferred giving simply does not outrank knowing something about imagery in Old Norse legends and knowing something about the initiation rites of Australian aborigines. An administrator refuses to understand this hierarchy of values of knowledge at the risk of incurring puzzlement, anger, even bitterness. And those who do understand it are understandably ever tempted to explain, even to themselves, all the reasons they are not at this very moment writing a paper on the image as signifier or on the effects of copper on the heart rate of bivalve mollusks.

Another campus cultural phenomenon that is closely related to class consciousness and that renders an academic
administrator subject to attacks of apologizing is the distance intellectuals attempt to place, and very often succeed
in placing, between themselves and the managerial class.
Take, for example, the manners of dress and the modes of
speech. Both groups "dress for success." They always have.
But whereas fifty years ago a campus visitor would have
found it difficult to distinguish a professor from an administrator by dress alone, since grey and brown flannel and
tweed was de rigueur for everyone, the intellectual upper
classes now affect a style that would rarely lead an outsider
to mistake them for members of a lower order. The favored
jeans and cords and bright flannel shirts and madras skirts
of the chemists and linguists are in sharp contrast to the
power blue suits and club ties and designer scarves of the
vice-presidents for administration and the deans of the
schools of business. Both the intellectuals and the managers
affect a style that consciously or unconsciously expresses the
distance between them. "I search for truth in dusty stacks,
while you attend power lunches," says one. "I attend power
lunches so that you can continue to sit searching for truth in
dusty stacks," says the other. The difficulty for administrators, in the context of these assertions, is that the first statement is most frequently uttered with pride, whereas the second one if often muttered in self-defense.

The language of higher education administrators, often
the target of humor and disdain as linguistic adventures in
academe, is often accompanied by self-consciousness and de-
fensiveness; the language of the disciplines, accepted as the
intellectual's necessary specialized rhetoric, is mastered
with self-confidence and a sense of being at home in an exclusive sub-culture. A Roland Barthes, influential sociologist
and lexicologist, could write, and be much admired for having written, a sentence such as the following: "It is probable,
as a matter of fact, that among the metabolas (or figures of
substitution of one signifier for another), it is metonymy
which furnishes the image with the greatest number of its
connotators; and that among the parataxes (or syntagmatic

figures), it is the asyndeton which predominates" (*The Responsibility of Forms*, Hill and Wang, New York, 1985, p. 39). On the contrary, when one talks of "working frameworks," "a conceptual rationale," "the correlating parameters," "the integration of disparate conceptualizations of career change," and "all managers' personal affective investment in their own thought structures," those who are still awake will envy those who are not. The reason for these differing responses to abstract language is simple. In the case of Barthes, the academic class structure views the study of semeiotics as demanding and worthwhile, whereas it considers the analysis of educational administration to have been encouraged for the purpose of feeding upon itself. In a word, the substance of the study of signs is worthy of its specialized vocabulary, however, esoteric, but in the faculty worldview, the matter of academic administration is too slight to support the accoutrement of its own locutions. Hence, academic administrative rhetoric, at times derided as "educationese," is dismissed as pretentiously obtuse and comically imitative of other specialized tongues. It wears a hat that covers its eyes and wobbles on high heels that were meant for adult disciplines.

While the significance of these contrasting styles of dress and language should not be exaggerated or overinterpreted, they are nevertheless sociological manifestations of the intellectual hierarchical tendencies on the modern campus and of the distancing among those belonging to one class or another.

Some faculties have, of course, distanced themselves from administrators in ways that carry more weight than dress and language. The formation of a bargaining unit, for example, will bear greater consequences for the relationship between faculty and administrators than will decorating one office with posters from the Bibliotheque Nationale and another with plaques of recognition from the American Chamber of Commerce. However, manners and style do make significant statements and do affect one's concept of self-worth and do create serious tensions in a culture as intellectually class conscious as that of academe. One neither remains ignorant of them nor succeeds in ignoring them with impunity.

Dicta that academic administrators choose to follow in seeking rapprochement with the faculty should include three elements essential to success. An administrator should cultivate a prose style that reflects clear thinking and respect for precision and individuality of expression. An administrator should spend as much time studying the broad concerns and advances of academic disciplines as he or she spends following the specific challenges and interests of managing contemporary colleges and universities. And, finally, an administrator should cease apologizing and seeking forgiveness for enjoying responsibilities that, when met with wisdom, energy, and creativity, make a significant difference in the biography of an institution.

The cultivation of a prose style that reveals an uncluttered but well-furnished mind and the pursuit of broad intellectual interests are at the mercy of an administrator's will and self-discipline. One decides to cultivate and to pursue or one decides, often by not deciding, not to cultivate and not to pursue. In both cases, the decisions are met alone; the solitary encounters and their aftermath are made known only at the discretion of the administrator though, of course, signs point to mountains climbed and not climbed. However, an administrator's decision not to adopt an apologetic or guilty stance is a communal matter, for the decision is spurred to begin with by expressions of dismissal or scorn for the essence of one's work.

It becomes clear that an administrator's response to the place assigned him or her by the faculty in the hierarchical world of the academy is more complex than that of an administrator's seeking a better understanding of his or her contribution to a common cause by keeping alive a respect for and interest in language and the disciplines. It becomes equally clear that one's work is adversely affected by a felt need to explain repeatedly why one decided to assault Everest by its Northern as opposed to its Southern route.

Under such circumstances, administrators have at least two choices. Some may find the confidence to look the academic hierarchy makers in the eye and to say once and only once, "I prefer to do this rather than that. Furthermore, my contribution to the common cause, while different from yours, carries it own significance of which I am proud." That kind of acceptance of self is, of course, the very core of freedom. All ease, humor, and perspective flow from it. It leads to a form of grace in which one is not embarrassed to express boredom before tax accountants who seek to describe exciting new ways of diversifying; where one is not brought low by the pettiness and chicanery of those who cling to the ways of childhood; where one is not affronted by critics whom one cannot please.

However, not everyone leans toward bold self-portraits. Others seeking to free themselves from a myth that paints them as unwilling victims of a fate that shanghaied them out of the classroom while they were in the middle of solving a mathematical conundrum may find grace elsewhere. Many administrators in search of lost time remember early dreams of emulating the learned professors who inspired visions of intellectual mastery. While their peers were eager to exchange the smell of chalk in classrooms for the aroma of soft leather in board rooms, they lingered for years in degree programs that finally allowed them never to leave the world of campuses at all. Now, as they meet in less well appointed board rooms, some voice within them may still sincerely be asking, though in ever fainter whispers, why they do not follow the dropped bread crumbs back home. While the answer in most cases is that home is no longer home, a gentler response might point to the forms of teaching in which all successful administrators engage.

A president who addresses an assembled chamber of commerce is teaching; a vice-president for academic affairs who leads a two-day seminar of deans is teaching; a dean who meets with the leaders of the student senate is teaching. And those administrators who care about teaching prepare these presentations with great care. For ignorance, disorganization, and superficiality in these teaching forums are weaknesses of the same magnitude and seriousness as they are in a credit-bearing chemistry or anthropology class.

Daphne Park, whose adventures as a British diplomat in such places as Moscow in the immediate post-Stalin years and in Ulan Bator in Outer Mongolia would likely fill the pages of a long and serious thriller, confessed that in later years as the principal of Somerville College, Oxford, "the hardest thing was to learn that I was regarded by the scholars as *only* an administrator, which is not necessarily to be greatly respected" ("Vital Powers," *New Yorker*, January 30, 1989, p. 71). Prejudices of the academy are apparently no respecter of geographical boundaries. However, Ms. Park and college and university administrators everywhere might remind themselves on cloudy days that the values of free speech, of open inquiry, of respect for those whose dreams are markedly different from one's own, of equal rights and opportunities for all, in sum, the values of the core curriculum are taught in multiple settings and in multiple ways. They are even taught by the decision making of administrators in navy blue suits who seek the principled and the lasting as opposed to the expedient and the ephemeral.

Play any tune, ride any horse, the brass ring in a university is always an enriched life of the mind.

OTHER VOICES, OTHER VIEWS

From the President of a Private College:

I did indeed long for the classroom for many years. In fact, for nearly a decade after becoming a full-time administrator, I still thought of myself primarily as a chemist. I would teach as often as possible and particularly missed the interaction with the students in the laboratory. As time went on, there was increasing difficulty in meeting the unforgiving schedule of the classroom and increasing difficulty in being available to the students for their extra concerns outside of the lecture hour. Finally, I cut the apron strings and have for ten years not been in the classroom on a regular basis.

There are, in my view, three reasons for my behavior:

1. Teaching is a very pleasurable activity. I enjoy the process and enjoy the response of the students to my teach-

ing. Obviously, I hesitate to give up such a pleasant experience.

2. Teaching can be a catharsis for an administrator. When you are in the classroom, none of the cares of the world can intrude. When the classroom door is closed the administrative slings and arrows are left outside.

3. We are all trained within a discipline and think of ourselves in that category for years and years. It is a very difficult habit to break. Also, thinking of oneself as "an administrator" is not as specific, clear, or even admirable as thinking of oneself as a chemist.

From the Dean of a Business School within a Public University:

I'm sure a few administrators genuinely miss being in the classroom and most of them probably return there eventually. A few more remember wistfully those stress-free hours spent talking with students over coffee about matters deep and profound. Almost all administrators envy their teaching colleagues for the time they have to pursue outside interests or to study a single issue or problem in minute detail.

So yes, this is probably a wise myth, but the word "classroom" is really a symbol for having enough time to do things the way you wish they could be done.

From the Vice-Chancellor of a Public University:

I suspect the yearning is not as widespread as we may wish to believe. This yearning is a function of a number of factors: One is the number of years the individual has been an administrator. The transition from the classroom to administration may be difficult in the early years of administration, but is likely to lessen with time. The yearning may return, however, when the administrator is experiencing difficulties and finds the administrative responsibilities unpleasant or unrewarding.

Further, it is fashionable, particularly in the early years of administration, to tell your colleagues on the faculty that you miss the classroom, even if you don't. They like to believe that administrators have deserted their true calling reluctantly, motivated by the desire to serve the institution more effectively or make more money. Longing to return to the classroom is good university politics.

Keep in mind, however, that no administrator is forced to remain in his or her position. The option to return to the classroom is always available should this yearning become overwhelming.

From the Provost of a Public University:

An administrator without this yearning (now and then) is probably in the wrong business. The reasons for going into higher education administration are complex and deserve study. But all of us feel a real loss when we depart from the classroom altogether.

From the Provost of a Private University:

Strangely, the major believers of that myth are my non-academic friends and parents of students, all of whom intone, "I bet you miss teaching." Far be it from me to say otherwise, but I'm no different than all of my faculty colleagues who expend all spare energy trying to get their teaching responsibilities reduced to as close to zero as possible.

From the Dean of a College of Arts and Humanities in a Public University:

If an administrator's primary goal is to seek higher administrative posts, then any such yearnings might need to be suppressed; however, if one expects to provide the best administration in a current position, one *needs* to teach at least occasionally.

As dean I was hearing combat stories from faculty and chairpersons about declining student writing ability, attendance problems, the effect of our withdrawal policy on learning, problems of classroom management, grade inflation, effects of the registrar's policies on record keeping, etc. I realized I needed to teach after a three-year absence from the classroom.

As a result, I am in a much stronger position advising faculty on how to deal with such matters and in finding improvements for policy changes. More importantly, I was reminded of why I earned a Ph.D. to pursue a career in higher education.

In order to teach and still do whatever a dean does, I appointed an "administrative intern" (one course released time) from the faculty to handle specific tasks which did not demand personal attention. In effect, I swapped some administrative tasks for a class. I recommend the idea to others who are happy in administration, but who *do* yearn for the classroom.

From the Vice-Chancellor of a Public University System:

This is a convention which ex-professors regularly proclaim. It is not a very credible effort to retain legitimacy among former faculty colleagues. Most senior administrators left the classroom because they wanted to work with intellectual peers and with real problems in real time. They will cherish memories of classroom successes and the successes of former students, but return to the classroom—never!

From the Vice-Provost of a Public University:

Virtually all academic administrators enjoy the privilege/ option of returning to teaching whenever they wish to. There are absolutely times when we all recall wistfully the best aspects of a teaching career. However, the salary differentials, the (perhaps sometimes imagined) increased prestige, and the feeling of being more involved in institutional policy development and implementation generally keep most of us doing what we are doing for many years.

From the Vice-President for Academic Affairs in a Public University:

When an administrator is given the opportunity to return to the classroom, he or she will miss the action and intensity of administration. The other job always looks better.

From the Provost of a Public University:

I suspect that such "yearning" largely has to do with the way in which the administrator sees herself. For example, what "path" did she follow into administration? If she came from a successful career as a scholar and teacher, did she enjoy the classroom part of her life? If so, then I suspect that some pull back to the classroom will always be there. If not, then the classroom will probably be viewed as a place best left behind forever. From a slightly different perspective, I believe that for the administrator who had a good classroom experience, this yearning is often motivated by a view of the classroom as a kind of intellectual sanctuary from the often dull routine of meetings that are so often the stuff of administrative life. Indeed, at many of these seemingly endless meetings, full of dull, dreary conversation, one can often dream Mitty-like of the hard-edged, professor-student give and take of the honors seminar, the tutorial, the upper-division course or graduate class in one's specialty and yearn and yearn some more. I know that I do! But, then, I loved my years in the classroom and the library and look forward to returning to both one day before retirement. Even now I "cheat" on my "provostian" time by teaching a class each year and making a valiant effort to stay current with the most important literature in my academic field. Count me with the minority, at least I think that it is a minority, who will "yearn for the classroom"—at least some of the time.

From the Dean of the College of Arts and Sciences at a Private University:

If an academic administrator does not "yearn for the classroom" from time to time, he or she is in need of soul searching about the perspectives being applied to academic administrative decisions. However, if an academic administrator yearns for the classroom all of the time, he or she has made a vocational mistake.

From the Provost of an Unnamed Institution:

Most discipline-based academic administrators came to administration because they were faculty leaders and had some stature as teachers. As a result, the classroom—especially after months of interminable meetings—remains an attractive ideal and a motivating principle. This has been my personal experience and my observation of administrators in liberal arts and comprehensive colleges. My experience in two research universities was very different, but, then again, "the classroom" was not terribly attractive to anyone there.

From the Dean of the College of Letters and Sciences at a Public University:

Perhaps "yearn" is too strong a word. This administrator fully expects to spend the last few years of his career in the classroom, as well as in the library and the laboratory. He has continued to teach throughout his nine years in academic administration and expects to continue this behavior for another 5–10 years. After that, it is back to the faculty—whether they want me or not!

From the Dean of a Branch Campus at a Public University:

Classroom, in this myth, is a metaphor for "safe haven," or "safety valve," or for a situation where one can feel more in control than one usually feels in university administration. No one I have known (including myself) has truly yearned for a return to the classroom.

From the Former Dean of a School of Law at a Public University:

While it is common to hear that administrators wish "to return to teaching" I think it is probable that what most *really* want to return to is the relative freedom and independence of the professorial life.

Throughout my own administrative years, I have maintained a teaching schedule (one class in most semesters). In that context, it certainly is true that I have "yearned" for more time to devote to the classroom activity, that is, preparation and research. I'm a good teacher (say my perhaps misguided students) and enjoy teaching, but I don't believe I've ever really missed it during administrative assignments (maybe because I've never completely left). The classroom provides certain stimuli, but so does administration.

From the Chancellor of a Public University:

Probably more truth to this myth than most, but the yearning will be manageable.

Administrators, like teachers, yearn for an audience—a classroom is a good one, but not the only one.

From the Dean of Arts and Sciences at a Public University:

For some, including me, this is not a myth—and this does not mean one has to do *either* administration *or* teaching; with some good planning and timing an administrator should be able to teach a course from time to time. In fact, all the positive things said about being in the classroom/laboratory environment have been true for me: the exhilaration of teaching/learning, even when it doesn't involve one's original specialization; keeping up to date in the area of one's discipline; being able to bring one's new experiences and insights to bear on problems; challenging and being challenged by students; gaining additional perspectives by witnessing firsthand the problems faculty and students have to bear in their everyday life at the university; turning one's attention briefly away from the regular "emergencies" seen by administrators; etc. In short, it adds spice to an exciting life.

From the Vice-President of a Private Liberal Arts College:

An administrator will find it expedient and flattering to faculty to "yearn for the classroom" in public pronouncements, to characterize himself or herself as only temporarily on leave from the academic frontline, and to speak in wistful and poignant tones of the good old days of preparation, lecturing, and the grading of papers. But in truth, in the deep and secret places of the heart hidden from the view of the tenured and the tenure-seeking, the administrator will often find welling up from within the inexpressible and unutterable thought that no matter how rough the squalls or how tearing the winds which beset, at least I don't have to go into the classroom every week and face those students.

The administrator left the classroom for good reason, most often after a hard-fought campaign of years of effort rivaling great and celebrated escapes from gulag, stalag, and camp the world over. Scratch the tweedy or pinstriped surface of an administrator and you discover beneath not the soul of a teacher dying to interact with students, but the burnished-steel central-processing unit of a person who wants to run things.

Chapter 5

An Administrator Who Has the Will Will Find the Way

Some years past, the *New Yorker* (December 24, 1984, p. 60) ran a short account of games played in Provence in the summer. One was called *taureaux pasteque* or *taureaux watermelon*. On the surface of things, it was a very simple game: each contestant had to eat a piece of watermelon while seated on a bench; whoever finished first won. The complicated part was tied to the fact that the bench was in the middle of a bull ring—as was the bull. One's chances of winning are always tied to the conditions under which one plays and the context within which one plays.

And yet, an administrator who listens closely to his or her harshest critics will hear the same thematic phrase sounded over and over again: the claimed inability to solve a problem is a bureaucratic euphemism for the unwillingness to solve a problem. A department's needs, for example, are very frequently described as standing in solitary splendor outside the context of space or time. A professor of French, who refers to administrators as *les gros legumes*, (*the big veggies*—a disrespectful version of *the big cheese*) once illustrated this attitude in a scene worthy of any institution's preserved lore. The dean of his small public university in a state not known for its generous support of higher education had refused to fund a new language laboratory on the grounds that the budget could not bear its projected $150,000 cost. With legs and arms a'flailing, the professor of French made it clear that the dean of the college of arts and sciences cared nothing for the department of foreign languages, for the decline of the study of foreign languages in the United States, for the improvement of international relations, and for the health of a global economy. His parting shot rang through the halls: "We will teach you, sir, that this is a university, not the marketplace where the bottom line determines decision making."

This and similar scenes repeated yearly on campuses everywhere seem to reflect the frustration of faculty and administrators alike of not being able to replace expensive outmoded equipment in one aging laboratory after another. However, beneath the surface of this discontent lies a phenomenon of greater interest than that of the struggle to make do with inadequate budgets. The French professor's accusation was clear and without qualification: the dean would not fund the new language laboratory because the dean did not *want* to fund the new language laboratory. Unless one takes the position that all faculty are by nature unreasonable outside the narrow confines of their disciplines, unless one accepts the proposition that all faculty believe that administrators are by nature perverse and, like Iago, revel in their own malignity, one must ask why intelligent, sincere, and generally well-meaning individuals would hurl such accusations.

One may begin to formulate an answer by examining the romanticism of the professorial calling. In a world of killing fields and gulags, apartheid and terrorism, faculty recite poetry and compose lieder and choreograph ballets. While legislative hearings drone their weary tale of corruption and deceit, faculty discuss the role of the church in medieval Provence; while explosives are tied to the underside of school buses in the Middle East, faculty explore the mysteries and wonders of the human cell. Semester after demanding semester and with mounting evidence to the contrary, they proclaim to each freshman class the grand possibilities of the human spirit. For the hundred-tenth time in the twenty-sixth year of a career that for most brings little worldly glory, they teach the normative ablative in Latin I and the origin of eating utensils in European History 102 in the belief that knowledge, even of dead languages and dead worlds, can catapult us beyond venality. Theirs is as romantic and courageous an enterprise as the writing of a sonnet about what it means to have escaped the Khmer Rouge. And the romanticism and the courage are not limited to those who are attached to the colleges of arts and sciences, but extend to the many in the professional schools who would lift the professions to the highest planes of human expectations.

Hence, to understand the idealism of the very nature of the academic profession is to understand the resistance to prosaic views and approaches that in the name of practicality and expediency and reasonableness threaten to erode the shores of an essentially romantic account of the way things are, or, at the very least, of the way things might be. One begins to see why the practices and the rhetoric of efficiency principles are feared as concepts destined to sabotage ideals that transcend the affairs of the moment. "I frankly resent having to talk about the cost of this program semester after semester. I'm a set designer, not an accountant." "The members of the legislature must simply be made to understand that the university is not the transportation department." "Since when are the credit hours produced the decisive factor in any regulation?" "It's unfortunate that only three students registered for Sanskrit, but I should be allowed to teach it anyway. Is this a university or a shoe factory?" "If this administration cared about the honors programs, it would find a way to build it its own house. Lip service is all we ever get from the president, and the dean doesn't really care, either."

Administrators hear such complaints several times a month, and it helps to understand their source. However, the romantic idealism of the faculty explains much more than its nearly always imaginative, at times excessive, and occasionally surly expectations of an administration constrained by very real if mundane limitations. In part at least, it also speaks to a faculty's disdainful dismissal of contemporary academe's managerial mania for attaching numbers to the appraisal of activities once thought of as belonging to a realm where quantification had been denied citizenship. And many faculty are less than sympathetic when senior administrators seem to succumb to the quantifying mania in the name of accountability. To measure the length of Don Quixote's spear and the speed of his horse and the strength of the windmill's blades is not only to snuff the life out of a poetically human effort, but in the long run is truly beside the point.

Chester Finn, in a piece called, "Judgment Time for Higher Education," (*Change*, July/August, 1988, pp. 35–36) defends generalizations about higher education. Arguing that one can generalize about any industry, he says that although "your local Burger King has about as much in common with La Cygne as Upstate Community College has with Princeton," this does not prevent us from commenting on the restaurant business, and by analogy, should not deter us from rendering universalized judgments on the "industry" of higher education. Faculty expect administrators to consider such analogies unfortunate, for they reveal as much about the author who creates them as they do about the correspondence between subjects under examination. Few in academe but the truly jaded would, for even an unguarded moment, think of higher education in industrial terms. And many who remember the size of their souls before the years spent in libraries and lecture halls and laboratories would find it at least mildly distasteful to have the enterprise placed somewhere between the restaurant industry and the aerospace industry because it absorbs approximately 2.8% of the Gross National Product. Administrators who do not find it distasteful may be doomed to misunderstand a faculty that can become enraged by assessment approaches that talk of "productivity" and "quality control" in the teaching of the classics as if the references were to productivity and quality control of hamburgers. Faculty, who hold to the traditional ideals of the academy, expect administrators not only to combat such vulgarity with vigor, but never even to appear to lose an inch of ground to the invading Goths whom they fear have already breached some walls. Indeed, the cynicism of some faculty is tied to the suspicion that administrators are secretly if not overtly sympathetic to the foes' values and are acting as double agents in an effort to sabotage their world.

Consequently, faculty reserve their deepest scorn for administrators who seem to give management more than its due: administrators who refuse to battle windmills and to chase white whales and to build cathedrals. In the faculty's study of the semeiotics of the managerial class, two signs in particular give rise to serious concern. First is the cliché philosophical posture that capitulates in the name of practicality and political wisdom to the "If we do not do it, they will" mindset. Clearly, the argument goes, the legislature will mandate assessment programs, so we had better protect ourselves by devising instruments to quantify the value of studying literature even when we are convinced that such testing fraudulently distills the essence of literature until nothing is left but aspects that lend themselves to measurements. Second is the cliché rhetoric that panders to the critics of higher education who accuse it of waste, mismanagement, and greed and that attempts to disguise a college or university as just another business enterprise that answers the immediate needs of the community: "learning outcomes," "productivity quotas," "faculty workloads," "plant usage," "administrative overhead," "quantitative evidence," "trial balloons," "windows of opportunity," "program marketing," etc. To refer to such barbarisms as "outcomes-oriented curricula" in a tone that congratulates itself for being avant-garde might be amusing if it were not so dangerous. Conscientious faculty have always cared deeply about the "outcomes" of their teaching and have always known that the effects of their lectures were rarely confined to the mastery of the subject matter that formed their content. One does not live by measurement alone.

To dismiss faculty contempt for such philosophical positions and industrial rhetoric as only to be expected from a smug, self-righteous, and arrogant intellectual establishment may make the harshest critics of higher education feel daring, but it hardly advances an understanding of academic culture. To characterize faculty insistence that administrators transcend the postulates of the age as extraordinarily naive may make presidents and deans feel worldly and wise, but it hardly helps to protect an environment that has for generations transmitted humanistic and civilizing ideals that deserve to be cherished.

A contemporary academic administrator walks daily through mine fields of irony. A faculty that considers itself slighted if virtually any decision is made without its having been consulted, nevertheless expects its president single-handedly to transform any opponent's value system. Then there are the off-campus critics of the academy. They judge the troubles of the late 1960s and early 1970s to have tested the depth of the administrative leadership's faith in the traditional values and central significance of the academy and to have found it wanting. Now, they unapologetically view the challenges of the 1980s as testing the leadership's openness to change and accuse it of promoting a blind faith in its institutions' inherent worth and of bowing low before the unquestioned conviction that an expansion of its systems should a priori become a national priority.

However, such ironies are not central to anyone's emotional life but that of an administrator whose responsibilities include knowing when to ride in groups, when to ride alone, and when to refuse to ride at all; knowing how much faith is too little faith or too much faith or no faith at all. In all cases, the campus constituency is apt to judge administrative decisions as acts of the will that meet or fall short of standards that are detached from considerations of expediency.

In *More Die of Heartbreak*, Saul Bellow writes that "when Herbert Spencer was asked how it was that after so many years of thought his forehead was unwrinkled, he answered that he had never been long perplexed by any problem." Barring communication with the ghost of Herbert Spencer, administrators must struggle to make clear that a university's life of politics is never as limpid as its life of the spirit—without for a moment implying that both lives carry equal value or denying that they are in some ways intertwined. An attempted aphorism that would read "Where there is a collective will, there may be a way" does not have much of a romantic ring to it; the trumpets are muted and few will be inspired to charge. However, while not recommending its use, one can recognize its truth.

Three approaches might lead to the establishment of an effective "collective way" by persuading a campus constituency that the administrative leadership is engaged in a common cause with its faculty.

One, presidents, vice-presidents and deans might in all their communications eschew the use of a rhetoric appropriate to the goals of commerce and industry, but out of keeping with the traditional ideals of a university. This alone would effect a significant rapprochement between the faculty and the administration on all campuses and persuade many skeptics that the leadership's will is attached to visions not dissimilar to their own. Professional jargon simply does not travel well. Everyone, including the most traditional and most idealistic faculty, understand on some level that fiscal sophistication is needed for the responsible allocation of multi-million dollar budgets. However, financial matters and their reporting need not be inextricably bound to a rhetoric suggesting to some that cost accounting has become, if not an end in itself, a priority that supercedes what it was designed to account. For example, rather than talking of "marketing research," one can speak of the knowledge and insights acquired by conducting research in the offices of academic advising and alumni and by listening closely to community advisory boards. And one most certainly should choose to refer to an institution's traditions as opposed to its product differentiation. In the academy the comfort level rises if references are made to the number of students who graduate; it lowers if the references are to greater productivity. What the academy seeks is high quality of instruction and research, not quality control; what the academy takes pride in are tasteful publications, not media blitzes or mag spreads.

Senior administrators who cultivate a jargon that shouts their sycophantic longing for what passes for worldliness on Wall Street and Madison Avenue are as embarrassing as an old woman in a mini-skirt. One does not know whether to lower one's eyes to the floor or lift them to the ceiling. For language does more than signify; it conveys that which is not made explicit. Hence, administrators should take great care that the words they choose reveal not only that which they intend precisely at any given moment, but that which they believe worthy of honor for all time.

Two, presidents, vice-presidents and deans might take the time to explain, in any number of forums and ways, that while efficient management is not a goal in itself, it must be achieved for the sake of supporting the very ideals that both faculty and staff share and wish to promote. Faculty who most often and quite appropriately manage nothing but their classrooms, their laboratories, and their publications, are surprisingly unaware of the university world outside the purely academic sphere. Since administrators spend a considerable portion of their own professional lives dealing with a campus's non-instructional divisions, they often mistakenly assume that all who are knowledgeable about chemistry and literature are equally well informed about the rising costs of operating bookstores and dining rooms. For example, while banning the use of the term, *make-buy*, one can nevertheless find opportunities to explain that in an effort to meet the high rate of inflation in the cost of library subscriptions, the university will henceforth contract with outside firms to provide security, or food service, or maintenance. Explaining the details of such decisions to a faculty in appropriate forums is time-consuming and runs the risk of attracting significant amounts of amateurish advice, but the knowledge that administrators do not limit their cost benefit analysis to faculty/student ratios is worth both the time and the risk when one considers the contribution that understanding can make to building a sense of confidence and common cause at any given university.

Additionally, anyone on campus whose requests for funds are denied should be given honest reasons for the refusal and for the support of other requests that have been given priority. To avoid setting priorities in a vain attempt to please everyone is virtually to guarantee mediocrity across disciplines and across supporting enterprises. However, to subscribe to this managerial dictum is not to have adopted the values of an alien culture, but to have simply admitted and honestly expressed what has always been true for all universities, that is, that none of them have ever been distinguished in all fields at all times. Willing a world that does not impose choices does not create one.

Three, Presidents, vice-presidents and deans might guard against giving the impression that meeting the short-term needs of a community constitutes the central mission of a college or university. An administrator's vision and will, while sensitive to the immediate needs of a region or a nation, must soar higher than the temporal demands of any geographical zone. A university must insist on educating not only for today, but for tomorrow, and it must also insist on its right to refuse the pursuit of mediocrity. While the industrial leaders of a region, for example, might conclude that they would profit from the public university's inaugurating a degree in manufacturing engineering technology, they would not profit from any but a good one. A good one is expensive and should not weaken the programs that are already established. A president must find the courage to tell them this diplomatically enough to retain their support. The growth of a healthy university is not analogous to the growth of a healthy business: the number of "clients" never plays an equally determining role. Few things undermine more surely the confidence of a faculty in its administration than the conviction, or even suspicion, that for political reasons its administration will sacrifice depth for breadth. Of course, senior administrators must remember a faculty's universal reluctance to conclude that any given program's level of funding support is such that the university can now afford to turn its attention toward a potential rival. It may be W. H. Auden who pointed out that man's tragedy is to want to be loved exclusively.

The point to keep in mind, however, is that to add or not to add programs is among the most complex and most serious of a senior administrator's decisions and one that may not always be given the reflection it deserves. For many a campus's weak sense of a common cause derives from a faculty's view that new programs are approved solely with "business" as opposed to "educational" ends in mind. Undoubtedly, regrets should often be forwarded when an all-too-eager acceptance is mailed. Once, Jean Cocteau, the French playwright, reportedly sent a telegram canceling a visit. It read: "Regret cannot come. Lie to follow." Administrators might do well to be prepared upon occasion to reverse Cocteau's *bon mot* and to send a telegram that reads: "Regret cannot meet request. Truth to follow."

These three suggested methods of establishing a common will in a university are, of course, in keeping with very sound business practices. Their application, through respect of language, shared governance, and time-tested managerial principles, simply takes into account a culture that differs in significant ways from all others.

Administrators who speak like CEOs of shoe factories; administrators who neglect to explain fiscal priorities; administrators who page through the Bureau of Labor Statistics data and worry that, in the manner of shoe factories, rice mills, and steel foundries, higher education productivity seems to be declining, will understandably be mistaken for CEOs of shoe factories, and rice mills, and steel foundries. They will, also understandably, be accused of lacking the will to resist those who for short-term gain would turn our universities into trade schools and skills centers whose productivity can be measured to the excited heartbeats of number crunchers.

Those who do have the will to resist the distortion of the splendid traditional mission of a university may, of course, not always find the way. But there is some incentive value to the myth that would claim otherwise: history will judge them on the extent to which they tried. The culture of the academy, for all its romanticism and its idealism—indeed, precisely because of its romanticism and idealism—keeps faith with all we might be if only we try. It ignores the limitations of space and time and encourages all who enter it not only to see, but to dream.

OTHER VOICES, OTHER VIEWS

From the Vice-President for Academic Affairs of a Public College:

> Can an administrator who has the will
>   find the way?
> When there is all rain and no sun
>   can a farmer make hay?
> When faculty positions are needed
>   and no funds are forthcoming
> It takes a pill, not will
>   to keep on humming
> When outgo is greater than income
>   and the Board takes rather than gives,
> When faculty are up in arms
>   and the administrators express disbelief
> The will has a helluva time
>   finding the proper motif
> In the realm of limited possibilities
>   wrought by the will of those in power
> Trying to find a way based on the will
>   always turns the sweet to sour
> When the farmer through FMHA discovers
>   how in the rain he can make hay
> The administrators will certainly confirm
>   that where there's a will there's a way.

From the Vice-President for Academic Affairs at a Private College:

Let me reverse the aphorism: an administrator who has the way will find the will. Resources breed ideas. Sometimes ideas breed resources, but in my experience that conception rate is considerably less than the reverse.

One difference between the academic and the administrative has become clear to me over the years. Ideas for their own sake are the meat and drink of faculty life. Ideas without the underpinnings of funds are death-rattles to an administrator.

From the President of a Public College:

I use to give this myth at least 80% credibility when I worked in the private sector of higher education. Of course, people had to be persuaded and motivated, resources had to be identified and secured and governance processes had to be followed. But it did seem that determination, hard work, focus, dedication, communication, and other lesser virtues did pave the way toward getting the most important agenda items done. Creativity, innovation and flexibility were often good substitutes for simple will.

Then I shifted to the public sector, and I now find it difficult to assign even token credibility to this myth. Circumstances abound which make "timing"—a critical dimension of good administration—next to impossible. Windows of opportunity slam shut before system and institutional machinery can crank into action. These circumstances may be bureaucratic impediments, union contract restrictions, fear of displeasing politicians, or the myopia of board members. These and related hurdles on the road to institutional accomplishment have led me more to believe in luck and fortuitous accidents than in force of will.

From the Dean of a School of Business at a Public University:

Administrators who adhere to this myth in all matters will soon find their way out of a job. Few activities terminate a career faster than the stubborn pursuit of objectives endorsed by no one else. I don't mean that administrators should surrender easily to louder voices or the ever-present lack of adequate resources. Instead we should be guided by that prayer which asks that we have serenity to accept the things we cannot change, the courage to change the things we can, and the wisdom to know the difference.

From the Provost of a Public College:

Two counter examples:
I have been an academic administrator in three different colleges for over fifteen years. In each, I have had a very strong desire to accomplish a reasonably simple objective: the evaluation of faculty teaching which would be sufficiently sophisticated to survive scrutiny in a sophomore level class in methodology. I have offered to put money, time, and other resources into the project. I have promised that if such an objective were to be reliably pursued, I could find money to support it from foundations, government agencies, and donors. I have also said that it would be the best way I know to displace excessive emphasis on research and publication in the process of the evaluation of faculty for tenure and promotion. I have willed it—oh, how I have willed it.

What have I gotten? Student questionnaires on student perceptions of faculty teaching. In my view, these have been correctly called "opinionnaires." They give some information, but not much of serious value and surely even the dullest student in a sophomore methodology course would know they do not provide an adequate basis for evaluating faculty teaching. What have I gotten beyond that? I do not wish to demean all else, but I would summarize it by calling it largely anecdotes. I have had the will. I have not found the way. The myth is just that: a myth.

Finally, I have also willed that people on campuses who are trained as scholars would not pass on rumors or unexamined myths, but they do, and I have found no way to stop it.

From the Provost of a Public University:

I learned from my step-father to talk about my dreams as if they were reality, and people will come to believe and then soon you have no choice but to make them real. I do believe many things can come to be through the force of belief and will of the leader. But not everything. It is important to know how to find a way to veer left or right, to go over the wall or dig under when necessary to get to your goal. However, sometimes the goal or the direction must be changed or abandoned. If it's a "sunk cause," let it go quickly and go on to the next goal. The will must be the mean, not the end.

From the Provost of a Private University:

There is some truth in the statement [myth], but it can easily be carried so far as to become an immediately closing tautology: if you didn't find the way, you must not have had the will.

There are many barriers that must be surmounted to get things done. Effort and ingenuity are often required in order to get around state and institutional hurdles, but one should not assume, explicitly or implicitly, that the only requisite to the solution of any problem is the will to identify a solution. There would be few problems if solutions depended only upon the desire that they appear.

From the Vice-Chancellor of a Public University:

As Bultmann has accurately stated, the process of demythologizing often leads to an empty set when all of the layers of the myth have been removed. I suspect that is the case with this myth. Based on my own administrative experience, it is "pure myth" and has no approximation in reality.

To subscribe to the myth personally, that is, to suggest that I have the will and therefore I will find the way, is to assume what I would call the "Ollie North" syndrome. Academic institutions are generally run on the "collective will" and it has been my experience that when a senior administrator routinely finds a "way" to realize his or her will at the expense of the "collective," he or she doesn't last very long.

From the President of a Public College:

In today's environment having the *will* and the *way* is not enough! Unless one also holds the *goodwill* of the campus community and at least general support for a project, grief is certain to follow.

From the President of a Private College:

Sure it's [the myth] true. But often at significant cost to the college and to that administrator's working relationships with colleagues and faculty. You *can* often do *whatever* you want providing you are not too "picky" about the means or about the long-run consequences.

From the President of a Private College:

This [myth] can be true *if* it means biding one's time until an idea dropped takes seed and starts to sprout. But if it means "come hell or high water," we'll do it my way, then the administrator is not likely to last very long in that particular position. Getting things accomplished requires some sense of ownership on the part of those being asked to change. Imagination, creativity, and a strong measure of patience can be valuable assets if one decides on this myth as an acceptable course of action.

Thus, I believe that there is an element of truth in this myth, and it is practiced in both of the ways mentioned above. I prefer the first way and abhor the second—but secretly envy some who by following the second route get things done more rapidly than I do. However, their workplaces are not very pleasant.

From the Provost of a Public University:

Almost all organizations have enough flexibility to allow for reallocation of resources and restructuring of units and responsibilities. An imaginative and resourceful manager is challenged rather than daunted by such constraints as limited budgets, tenured and not very flexible faculty, and inadequate facilities. Part of the reason some people enjoy the challenge of management (*not* administration) is precisely because it provides opportunities to match one's wits against various obstacles. In that sense, it is true that most of the time those who have the will also find the way(s).

From the Provost of a Private University:

There's enough truth in this statement to take it out of the myth category. After all, hard work and good planning do make success more likely. I would restate it to say: if you have the will, the patience of a saint, a sense of humor, and courage, you might win a victory now and then.

From the Chancellor of a Public University:

You *can* find a way to get things done. The best way to make it happen is through moral persuasion or other subtle means. It has become apparent to me, in a state system with an incredible bureaucracy and a great deal of political influence, that there are still ways to get things done. They might not be the obvious ways and the ways one would most like to follow, but they do exist. When you are new to the system and new to the bureaucracy, it takes some time to find that out. But I found that finding those ways is enormously important and that you usually can find that way if you listen and persist.

From the Dean of a Public College:

Up to a point, sure. There is a lot that can be done with charisma, just bringing a new style, helping expectations to rise, encouraging others, etc. However, if you don't get any support from central administration, or the system, or the president or whomever, after a point you had better leave. You risk damaging your own credibility if, after all the good ideas and planning, you can't convince anyone to support your plans. Or if they get squashed for dumb bureaucratic reasons. This support doesn't have to be everything you ask for, but it does have to be something. The trick is to figure out when to go if you don't get it.

Chapter 6

An Administrator Will Equivocate

In *The Divine Comedy,* Dante employs some of his most intentionally repulsive metaphors in describing those whom Justice on earth "had found to falsify." In some pit of the Inferno, their shrieks and tears are "as arrows all so barbed with grief" that the narrator must, with both hands, close his ears. They lie on their bellies and are heaped across one another's backs, for many cannot lift their bodies from the ground. From head to foot they are encased in scabs and each plies "the bite of his own nails for the great rage of itching" without finding succor. Their nails draw down the scabs as a "knife might scales from bream" or some other fish.

Thirteenth-century Italy, in theory if not in practice, did not waver regarding the evils of deception and what should be done to those who indulged in it. With the passage of time and the change of venue, certain of the educated seem to have been stricken with blurred vision, and in our time and place some of the proposed cures are as appalling as the disease. In a recent piece in *Common Cause Magazine* (P.M., "The Path of Sleaze Resistance," May/June, 1988, p. 8), we learn that "the nation's ethics shortage" has given rise to the country's newest profession: "ethics entrepreneurs." Associations and centers are "packaging" seminars and conferences on the question of ethics and at least one workshop, carried the title, apparently with no intended humor, "Before All Hell Breaks Loose: How Senior Executives Can Protect Themselves in Ethical Situations." General Dynamics has set up an ethics hotline and the University of Virginia's Darden School of Business has offered a seminar that promised to "demystify" ethics presumably for those who find it a matter of mystery.

It is of interest to note that as judged by the brochures that come across one's desk, the topic of ethics is the topic of truth. The implication in all advertisements for these seminars and institutes is that the sin of choice for those in power is clearly "the lie." Hence, in this context the words, *ethics* and *truth* are virtually interchangeable. This comes as no surprise, since most persons in positions of responsibility are now engaged primarily in processing *the word:* in providing or withholding accurate or misleading information and judgments and evaluations. In that sense, the power of words has increased with the increased power to transmit them through space and time.

However, one needs a heavy carapace of cynicism not to be surprised by the implied depth of culpable ignorance and vulgar unconcern many professionals have heretofore shown for the nature and complexities of truth as evidenced by the jejune titles and sophomoric descriptions of the content of workshops and institutes offered defense contractors, business chief executive officers, journalists, and government staffs. The level of discourse suggests a level of ethical illiteracy that consigns *The Divine Comedy* to the occult.

Even if such obtuseness were limited to professions outside the academy's walls, one would derive little comfort since the leaders of business, industry, and government have been educated within American higher education's grounds. Furthermore, the cavalier treatment of honesty by a significant number of high-level university administrators in such areas as intercollegiate athletics, personal expense accounting, and the lowering of academic standards have persuaded many that leaders of academe would be bold, indeed, to imagine themselves on some high ridge looking down.

It is both enlightening and sobering to consider that the one theme running through the long musical score of letters that reach an administrator daily—be they intended to express pleasure or pain, that of gratitude for truth—is played over and over again. No one finds it necessary to express gratitude for honorable behavior in other moral spheres; no one thanks a president or a dean for not absconding with the alumni annual fund or for not seducing the registrar, but many thank administrators for being forthright. "Thank you for being honest" or "I appreciate your honesty" constitutes a central refrain through many an interchange.

In a recent British television program called "South Bank," Doris Lessing, a prominent and thoughtful novelist not given to outrageous pronouncements, unequivocally stated that all politicians lie at all times and under all circumstances, that nothing they say is true—ever. Now, Doris Lessing, an intellectual who understands full well the nature of prejudice and the irresponsibleness of promoting it, nevertheless does not hesitate to dismiss before an audience on both sides of the Atlantic all members of an entire profession as by nature unethical. Likewise, a disproportionate number of faculty and students, otherwise fair-minded and tolerant and not known for pinning labels on entire categories of people on the basis of professional calling, will in all innocence and without an emotional clue as to their subtext, say of an administrator: "Well, it may be hard to believe, but he appears to be honest."

To come to an understanding of how we in colleges and universities have reached that spot is undoubtedly an appropriate subject for a full-length sociological study. For, without indulging in nostalgia about when ivy grew on hallowed walls, the history of higher education does not immediately conjure up visions of Robber Barons and Tammany Halls. However, any such study might well include an examination of five aspects of life on a contemporary campus that are certainly not unrelated to a complete knowledge of how we have arrived at this unintended and most frequently chimerical destination.

One is the nature of the curriculum. A curriculum that infrequently asks students to consider the ethical dimensions of all human acts within the context of all the disciplines not only deprives students of being fully aware of the moral dimensions of their decisions. It also creates an ambience on campus that fails to encourage those who are outside its classrooms from keeping well within the range of their attention not only the effectiveness but the honorableness of their own decision making. Responsible and energetic academic administrators remain *au courant* of the major questions that engage the attention of the university's various departments; and a university that does not through its disciplines focus some attention on the ethical concerns attached to its studies contributes to a campus culture where its community members, administrators, faculty, and students alike, become over time unaware or disengaged, and even uncaring, of the codes of civilized behavior that are in virtually all instances based on a search for truth and a love of truth.

The second is the spirit of competition. One would be hard pressed to point to any contemporary campus phenomenon that has eroded the dedication to truth, the core of an academic institution, more effectively than a spirit of competition that has grown at an alarming rate and that threatens to remain unchecked in the coming decade. Competition for academic recognition, for students, for athletics awards, for public and private funds, for kudos and honors and simple attention have scored one knock-out blow after another against truth. Media experts touch up glossies for catalogues; development officers inflate the worth of gifts in kind; publicists pump air into the reputation of faculty; and virtually everyone participates in exaggerating the accomplishments of students who apply for admission, who manage to remain attached to institutions that make modest intellectual demands, and who all too often graduate with little commitment to the life of the intellect.

The third aspect is the need for entertainment. One re-

cent fancy at baseball and football games is known as *the
wave.* Spectators in consecutive sections, beginning at one
end of the stadium and ending at the other, stand and raise
their arms while putting forth a verbal hum that is presumably meant to suggest vaguely the sound of a wave. This phenomenon is symbolic of an age when text (the game) is not
enough. It must be projected upon a screen and lit up in
flashing neon lights. Many a university has been infected by
this malady, an embarrassingly tasteless one, and engages
in all kinds of behavior indicating its loss of faith in the un-
adorned game. Since the community goes ho-hum when reminded of the elegant and distinguished traditional mission
of a university, one administrator after another engages
"teams" to adorn and highlight campus programs with the
intention of keeping everyone awake. The difficulty is that
these sideshows, ranging from costly alumni and athletic
hoopla to social service by-roads taken in response to a community's immediate needs, keep everyone's attention di-
verted from the truly important aerial acts in the main tent.
They deceive many into forgetting that the only purpose of
a university is to discover the truth and to teach it and to
preserve it. Even more dangerously, these diversions support those who are made happy by being encouraged to forget the mainline purpose.

The fourth aspect is frenzy for collaboration. Many
would agree that in a knowledge-intensive society, in which
national economic growth is dependent on an educated citi-
zenry and the success of all individuals is tied in ever more
complex ways to intellectual accomplishments, universities
should be making every effort to provide opportunities for
access that were denied to many in the past. Many would
also approve of working cooperatively with government and
business for the general welfare of all communities and, ultimately, for the nation. However, to suggest that universities
have not contributed significantly to the nation by serving
the ends of distant and non-partisan inquiry, or that this recent rapprochement with government and business has not
already exacted a price is a dangerous leap that may land
one in quicksand. One witnesses in many quarters an obse-

quiousness, a false humility, an unbecoming and eager description of the death of academic monasticism from which one wants to avert one's eyes. The values of the academy do not match in all respects the values of any other enterprise and those who represent the academy should not subscribe to words or deeds that would indicate otherwise. Collaborations are good and even necessary, but collaborations that are bought at the price of a dishonesty that mimics the values of bottom lines and yearly reports to the stockholders are collaborations that are overpriced. Many a faculty member has come to fear that a president's heart reserves a larger chamber for the good will and welfare of potentially generous regional companies than for the well-being of the core curriculum and the honors program. Many a student has come to suspect that those who purport to lead colleges and universities are not as disturbed by the growth of a preprofessional training that feeds the immediate needs of the economy at the expense of a more leisurely liberal arts education as the rhetoric of their convocation and commencement addresses would lead listeners to believe. These fears and suspicions, however wide of the mark, continue to water the growth of mistrust.

The fifth aspect is the semeiotics of architecture and design. Buildings are, but buildings and their contents also mean. In 1988 the University of Bologna celebrated its ninth centenary. Those in this country invited to its festivities received a handsome text written in both Latin and English summarizing the highest of its intellectual achievements of the past nine hundred years and featuring throughout photographs focusing on details of its magnificent courtyards, iconography, ceilings, walls, college emblems, even anatomical drawings from its Institute of Anatomy. While one was suitably impressed by the long traditions and accomplishments, one was also struck by the authenticity of the settings and their content: terra-cotta did not pose as marble; faded frescoes had not been touched up in Walt Disney vivid color. Indeed, in one especially telling photograph, that of the statue of Hercules that stands in the courtyard of the seat of the University of Bologna, the wall of the Palazzo Pozzi that forms the background exposes six windows with orange/red shades drawn now half-way, now a quarter of the way down, and at least two in obvious need of repair. In a word, the viewer knows that should he or she knock, there is somebody home. Furthermore, one need not touch the shades to feel certain they are not made of polyester.

In the aggregate, we have not as colleges and universities been overly sensitive to the contribution to truth that authenticity in the architecture of our buildings and the design of their contents can symbolize. Out of inattentiveness rather than with malice aforethought, we have not banned from our campuses false marble, plastic bamboo trim, and styrofoam wooden beams. We tolerate, or have ceased to see, artificial plants, waxed fruits, and fake early American furniture if not fake medieval facades. While one might find amusement in debating the advantages and disadvantages of living in an age when we really cannot be certain whether she does or does not dye her hair, we have perhaps been too cavalier in allowing the display of the fake and the artificial. We may have, thereby, contributed to the myth that decision makers do not value authenticity.

No institution, not even a university with its dedication to objectivity in teaching and research and its traditional pursuit of the truth, remains uninfluenced by the culture of its time and place. Hence, a modern campus ambience, in imitation of the society beyond its quad, seems at times amoral, overly competitive, hungry for the frivolous, inappropriately impressed by the manners of the world of business, and welcoming of the false in its structures. Critics will understandably accuse the leaders of higher education for, if not actually being false themselves, ironically creating the false impression that they might be.

Philosophers have struggled with the nature of the true and the false since the beginning of recorded history. Augustine, for example, distinguished among eight different ways of lying, and Thomas Aquinas divided falsehoods into the officious, the jocose, and the mischievous. Though only the naive would claim that presidents, vice-presidents and deans have never sinned in the formulaic ways outlined by either Augustine or Aquinas, the vast majority of senior academic administrators are honest and honorable people who take very seriously their primary responsibility to truth under all circumstances. Those who lie for useful or harmful ends only very rarely reach the ranks of senior administrators; those who manage to do so even more rarely outlast professionally the harm they do.

However, though very few administrators deliberately deceive, a few of the more inexperienced or less wise do upon occasion make the mistake of either placing some information, some knowledge, in exaggeratedly elegant settings before transmitting it to others, or of placing it in a vault and not transmitting it at all. Such behavior is usually spurred by one of four causes.

The first is kindness. The administrator knows that a message will hurt and employs so many euphemisms and circumlocutions in delivering it and follows so many irrelevant byroads in reaching it that misunderstandings arise. For example, a dean who meets with an instructor to complain about his teaching cushions the blow with such exaggerated praise of the instructor's research that the latter leaves the encounter not certain whether the purpose of the meeting was to fault his teaching or to commend his scholarship. Since the pleasant is easier to revisit than the unpleasant, the instructor discards the vague references to the need to improve his teaching and files for safe keeping the accolades bestowed upon his publications. Two years later, he is shocked and outraged when the dean recommends against granting him tenure, He accuses the administrator of having deliberately and callously deceived him and mistrust infects his supporters on the faculty and staff.

The second cause is enthusiasm. The administrator so lives in the strategic plan of a university that his or her descriptions reflect the university of the imagination rather than the university that may or may not in time be transformed by the dreams. For example, a vice-president for academic affairs who is eager for the college of business to encourage its students to study foreign languages begins preliminary discussions with the deans of the college of busi-

ness and the college of arts and sciences. Since the response
to the hope of hundreds of marketing students becoming flu-
ent in Russian, Japanese, and Chinese is positive indeed, the
vice-president is confident that all obstacles will eventually
fall. Within weeks there is some slippage in the accuracy of
her rhetoric and those who are inclined to inattention when
academics speak might be left with the impression that the
thought had already fathered the deed. When the answer to
a question reveals that the coals had been lit, but that nothing as yet had been broiled, the chef is viewed with suspicion.

The third cause is secrecy. The administrator, knowing
that timing is one of the most critical agents in the success
or failure of an enterprise, waits too long to reveal plans that
affect many. For example, the president of a small public
university, in an effort to avoid controversy while the appropriations committee of the state legislature is in session,
withholds temporarily from the faculty a budgetary request
for the expansion of a controversial interactive television
program which he himself values. This line item draws the
attention of Professor Z's brother-in-law, a staff member of
the appropriations committee, who informs Professor Z that
the one program he has worked for five years to abolish may
receive additional fiscal support. The president is accused
of deception by omission and his credibility among certain
faculty activists is irreparably damaged.

The fourth cause is neglect. The administrator, awed by
the time and effort that would have to be allotted to making
clear a complex matter, mistakenly oversimplifies an issue
and its potential consequences. For example, a dean of the
college of education who wishes to follow the recommendations of the Holmes Group Report decides after a restful
summer holiday to attempt to eliminate the undergraduate
degree in elementary education and to require all students
who plan to teach young children to major in one of the arts
and sciences. During the long and, at times, acrimonious debates that follow the announcement of this proposal in the
college of education, the dean assures his own faculty that
he is deep into planning with the college of arts and sciences

for the smooth transition of this major event should it be approved. Furthermore, they need not have a moment's concern that any of those outside the college of education who will be affected by this curriculum change envision difficulties that cannot be resolved. In actuality, the dean's "deep planning" has consisted of lunch with the dean of arts and sciences during which both agreed that the curricula and fiscal implications of this proposed reform would require serious study. The faculty of the college of education approve the proposal by a small margin. Then, nothing happens except that some members of the faculty no longer speak to certain colleagues. The dean, de-energized by the struggles within his own college, had avoided meeting similar ones elsewhere and had sought surcease from the pain of anxiety and fatigue by watching the World Series, Monday night football, and virtually every game of a winning Lakers season. The ending of the tale? Well, the provost considers a half-proposal worse than no proposal; the academic senate suspects a nefarious intent; the dean of the college of arts and sciences, who was waiting for a detailed plan before bringing it to her faculty, is unjustly accused of secrecy; the college of education faculty charges its own dean of exaggerated claims as to the university's readiness for and approval of this act of reformation.

These four all-too-human modes of behavior, all of which contribute to keeping alive the myth that all administrators by nature equivocate, have one alluring bait in common: ease. When traversing a week that begins to look like a cobwebbed path and the mosquitoes are biting, the sun is hot, and you have just tripped over a fallen branch and skinned your knee, it is exceedingly tempting to head for the cool clearing that lies just beyond making someone feel better than he or she perhaps should; by transposing what is into what will be; by withholding that which is certain to wake an opposition that may be napping; and by substituting the simple for the complex.

Of course, every experienced administrator knows full well that one nearly always succumbs to ease at one's own peril. The ultimate kindness is the truth. The conditions that will be improved are those recognized as corresponding to the truth. The plans that will be supported are those openly seen as the truth. The complexities that will be mastered and not resented are those that are explained as the truth.

It is neither too grand nor too elevated a statement to insist that a college or university's mission to protect and to honor truth is distinguished precisely because it thereby protects and honors civilization itself. It is neither too unworldly nor too unsophisticated to insist that, minor human failings aside, American universities would not have reached their present level of international esteem if the majority of its senior administrators had not revered that mission and had not understood in depth their responsibilities within it.

OTHER VOICES, OTHER VIEWS

[The above essay assumed that attempts to evade, to hedge, and to waffle were not unrelated to deliberate efforts to deceive. Many of the commentators, however, insisted that the line between the two meanings of equivocating was not too fine to draw.]

From the President of a Community College:

Ouch! Yes. All really good administrators leave themselves an out! Webster's first definition of the term includes intentional deception; his second definition speaks to avoidance of commitment. From my perspective, we tend toward the latter, not the former. At least, this is the case for me. I rarely deliberately lie. However, I not infrequently feel that I do not have adequate information or that I want to reflect further on an issue and avoid making a commitment until I feel adequately informed and have had enough time to think. Equivocation in the second sense is frequently taken to be equivocation in the first sense by those around you. Your lack of willingness to commit coupled with your perceived authority results in many feeling that you really do have an answer or decision, but are not revealing it. They may feel shut out or manipulated. I try to handle this by making clear what issues I need to consider further and at what time I intend to be unequivocal.

Over time, it becomes increasingly difficult to avoid the charge of equivocation. You see the same circumstances in a different way. Reconsideration of an issue in a very different context may produce a different decision on your part. You may just plain change your mind. Those about you rely on your consistency. They feel unsafe when they feel uncertain. This calls for efforts on our part to minimize equivocation, manage it well, and acknowledge that it is part of the administrative experience.

From the Dean of a College of Business at a Public University:

An adminstrator who communicates in ways deliberately designed to deceive others won't last long in academe. Statements from deans, vice-presidents, and presidents travel inside and outside the university with a speed which only light rivals. You are guaranteed to get caught and, if you're like me, having to chew your own words leaves a very bad taste in your mouth.

From the Assistant Vice-President for Academic Affairs at a Public University:

Every human who deals with areas of uncertainty equivocates, at least in the sense that statements and responses to questions—in order to be accurate—must reflect the levels of ambiguity present in the context within which the statement is made. Administrators in institutions of higher education must constantly work within interlocking systems of interdependent ambiguity: student and faculty behavior, the often unpredictable decisions of those beyond the institution (legislators, boards, alumni), even the performance of the stock market. Their plans and projections must realistically reflect that ambiguity. Certainly any successful administrator both recognizes the need for and creates the tolerance for flexibility: in this sense, he or she equivocates.

Administrators' stock in trade is information/knowledge. The best administrators successfully couple their knowledge with their wisdom to produce action in the best interests of their institutions. However, wisdom is of little value if it has not information with which to proceed. Consequently, an administrator tends to guard jealously his or her store of information while trying to elicit information from others to add to that store. The administrator who "knows the most," that is, has elicited more information than has been given away, tends to be the most successful. Does this situation tend to lead to equivocation in the second sense— to deliberately mislead? Obviously. This works a particular strain on the faculty-administration relations because the faculty member, by training and generally by inclination as well, sees information as a commodity to be shared and is often perplexed and angered when such expectations are frustrated.

From the President of a Public University:

There is some truth in the statement [myth]. However, I believe it to be either an exaggerated characteristic of the excellent administrator (he or she will occasionally hedge or be ambiguous) or a normal characteristic of the poor administrator.

In my own case, I occasionally resort to equivocation because I will try to avoid being pulled into someone else's fight.

From the Dean of the College of Natural and Social Sciences at a Public University:

Of course! Who doesn't? I do not, however, regard the administrator as more prone to this than others of his species— (speaking generically) including faculty members. Sometimes it may seem that the administrator is unduly equivocating because he is faced with so many more decisions than others on campus. The administrator should often buy time to think about the ramifications of his decisions and often to consult. The faculty member or student looming across the dean's desk is there because he (equally generic) knows that he is absolutely right and there are not two sides to the question. The dean who insists on investigating to see if there might be another side is therefore resented and perhaps regarded as an equivocating wimp. Have I equivocated?

From the Vice-Chancellor for Academic Affairs of an Unidentified University:

It is true largely because decisions often must be made before all facts are in and because every situation has another side to it which is often not known early enough. But what some would see as "equivocation" is often a matter of open-mindedness and sensitivity. The other side of equivocation is blind rigidity.

From the Chancellor of a Public University:

The temptation to equivocate is a strong and great temptation. I hope that it's not something most of us do very often. It is not an image that we can afford to have. It is much better to have met with as many groups and listened to as many people before the event as possible so that your decision, once made, is final. It is not good to have a reputation as someone who can be persuaded to change his or her mind.

From the Dean of the Branch Campus of a Public University:

A former chancellor I knew never put anything of consequence in writing—literally never. His face-to-face conversations were normally without witness, his public utterances most often mystifying. Did he equivocate? Not in writing, surely. Not in private conversation (though he did tell lies). His public utterances? I believe he did, but he would vehemently deny it because he did not intend to deceive by what he said while admitting what he did not say might be deceiving.

Administrators whose behavior I have observed in a

range of settings have equivocated if the term is taken to mean not always committing oneself through what one says at any point in time. This non-committal, I think, is critical to a decision-making process that seeks consensus. But at some point this process ends. The better administrators know it; the poorer ones seem never to learn it.

If equivocation by definition includes "an intent to deceive," it is a myth only if it is assumed by the word "will" that all administrators will do so. I have known many who have not done so, some under the most trying circumstances.

From the President of a Public University:

I am tempted to respond that all administrators *will* equivocate except for me. From the standpoint of petitioners, I am certain that *all* administrators equivocate. I am also certain that many administrators equivocate needlessly and frequently. An aspect of administrative wisdom is probably knowing when to equivocate, but most (I expect) err on the side of caution more often than on the side of risk taking. The latter, however, are in my judgment the superior administrators.

From the Provost of a Private University:

The term, equivocate, has two quite different meanings: (1) to make an intentionally deceptive statement of commitment, and (2) to avoid making commitments. I address each in turn.

1. I have only once in twenty years of administrative positions made a commitment I subsequently had to break, and that was because I failed, once, to read my administrative latitude and committed a resource I was subsequently prevented from allocating. It was an enormous surprise when that happened, and engendered an exhaustive apology and explanation to the person—a department chair—to whom I made the commitment. I don't remember at this point exactly what the resource was—probably permission to use a campus facility or something similar—but the re-

source preempted was not of great consequence and the department chair was able to accept my apology gracefully.

Other than the above instance, I have never retracted a commitment I agreed to, and know that those with whom I have worked have come to understand that my word, once given, is solid. To me it is absolutely essential that this be true.

2. I avoid making commitments that I cannot keep. Most of the time, the problem is that the person making the request asks for something I cannot commit. The administrative challenge is to see whether the request can be redesigned so that it covers something I am able to commit. For example, the request is for a new full-time staff position (which is unavailable). Perhaps the need can be filled by some temporary help.

The concomitant of a policy that avoids commitments one cannot keep is one that prevents you from being able to say an unambiguous "yes" to a request. My own strategy is to explain why I cannot at that point make a commitment—what the factors are that need to be clarified, what prior decisions have to be made, etc. The result can be protracted mini-lessons in administrative procedure, but on the whole the petitioner goes away with some sense of what the request entails, when a decision may be attainable, and whether my support is part of the process.

Uncharitable individuals will be no less inclined to assume that my word cannot be relied upon than if I really did equivocate. However, the majority of the faculty generally seem to feel a reasonable amount of trust in my commitments.

From the Dean of Arts and Sciences at a Public University:

Equivocation may be either apparent or real. Apparent equivocation may reflect uncertainty in the face of complex issues, or the evolution of an administrator's views as new dimensions of an issue emerge. Apparent equivocation is common enough in administrators, especially when we succumb to the temptation to state our positions with conviction without full information on hand.

Real equivocation differs in having as its goal the coloring of one's views, or of the truth, to appeal to the listener or to avoid commitment. When I was thinking about entering administration, I sought the wisdom of a respected colleague who was chancellor of a large state university. He offered only one piece of advice: Tell the truth as you understand it, and always tell the same story to everyone. I continue to regard this as the best advice I've ever received about administration. An administrator *may* equivocate; an academic leader will not.

From the Dean of a College of Communication at a Public University:

Equivocate, hedge, pussyfoot, beat about the bush, shuffle, dodge. Do administrators do these things? Sure. Why? Because they are trying to balance a variety of constituencies. Because policies are vague. Because they are unsure about support from above. Because our society is so litigious. Because most questions are not black or white. Is equivocation bad? Yes, no, maybe.

From the Dean of a College of Liberal Arts at a Public University:

Equivocation is often the charge hurled by faculty who didn't hear the answer they wanted to hear to their question.

However, "plain speaking" is not always the virtue it's cracked up to be. Certain truths spoken too baldly can demoralize rather than motivate, and may in fact produce a fearful clinging to the status quo rather than the growth and change the administrator is trying to effect. As my grandmother used to say, "Vinegar doesn't catch flies."

Administrators are constrained to observe rights of privacy and rules of confidentiality, and therefore cannot say everything to everybody. Furthermore, we all know that some of our interlocutors are more discreet than others and can be trusted with more sensitive information. At what point does tact or discretion become equivocation? Comfort

isn't a clue, because being tactful and discreet is often un-
comfortable (in fact comfort might sometimes be the clue
that one was doing the *wrong*, because easier, thing).

We may always be accused of equivocation, but I think
we do best to act and speak in such a way that we are always
confident that we are treating both people and information
with respect.

Chapter 7

An Administrator Will Be Torn by Conflicting Constituencies

The artist Marcel Duchamp's response to the assertion that he had abandoned painting for chess was both characteristically idiosyncratic and perceptive: "Just because a man starts to paint does not mean that he has to go on painting. He isn't even obliged to abandon it. He just doesn't do it anymore" (*Vanity Fair*, September 1988, p. 220). Though in this case what is true for the artist is perhaps true for the academic administrator as well, a Jamesian *ficelle* running through the compulsive explaining of those presidents and deans who leave administration, who "don't do it anymore," attaches itself to nearly every reason given for what some may view as abandonment. Over and over again one hears that the demands, at times conflicting, of faculty, students, parents, alumni, staff, classified employees, politicians, federal and state agency heads, and heads of business and industrial firms simply cannot be met to the satisfaction of everyone, even at the sacrifice of one's personal life and health.

Those who have taken the spurs off their boots smile knowingly and sympathetically when a president who is still riding broncos shares the following illustrative anecdote, the details of which have been altered to protect the guilty, but whose imagined points remain salient and "true." A mid-size public urban university in great need of classroom and office space to help meet the expansion of higher education following World War II solved its problem in what came to be seen as the accepted way: it installed two surplus army barracks on a vacant lot, painted them in an institutional color, planted begonias around their edges, and assured everyone that they were temporary. Forty years later, junior faculty, valiantly and more or less cheerfully attempting to feel as if they had finally joined the ranks of an honored profession, are still seated at battered desks in the barracks' drafty rooms. The legislature is not noticeably sympathetic to their plight and there is quite literally no place to which these faculty can move anywhere on campus or within reasonable distance off campus.

Enter stage right the fire department whose chief condemns the barracks as hazardous and unfit for occupancy. At that point all spectators climb onto the stage. To demolish a building in the state in question requires the permission of eleven agencies, all of which must "sign off" for the university to comply with the order of the fire department. These agencies range from the Dig Safe Center of the local telephone company to the Rodent and Asbestos Inspection Division of the state Department of Planning and Urban Development. Other "sign offs" are not quite as literal, but every bit as real. The alumni, who now remember that they have fond memories of spending many an hour chatting with faculty in one of the barracks' common rooms, begin to feel rather sentimental about drabness and wish they had been involved in the decision to destroy a part of the institution's history. The senior faculty reminisce about what it meant to be a faculty member at this institution when everyone knew everyone else and struggled together and had a common cause and faculty were not effete yuppies who were concerned or even aware of the color of window shades and presidents were scholars and not public relations experts concerned above all else with appearances. The junior faculty housed in the barracks would much prefer to stay there indefinitely if the only alternative is time-sharing already cramped offices occupied by others who refuse to remove some of their books from filled bookshelves. The student senate resolves that an empty lot gives the university an abandoned look. The chair of the neighborhood council fears that the empty lot will now attract squatters who have been setting up and living in tents in other parts of the city as a protest against the high cost of housing in the area. The letters that reach the desk of the vice-president for administration would easily qualify for the *New Yorker's* filler: "Letters We Never Finished Reading." The president is pleased to be reminded that we pass this way but once.

Of course, senior college and university administrators have always had multiple constituencies and have always arbitrated conflicts endemic to the assembly of humans in small and large institutions alike. However, the meaning of "constituent" and the meaning of "pleasing" an academic institution's expanded constituency has, in the past forty years or so, undergone an ever-increasing democratization that has made the governance of universities far more complex, far more demanding, than it ever was in the past. The ex-cathedra statements, the fiats, the paternal/maternal gestures, the patronizing from on high have all gone the way of the dodo bird. A certain hauteur characteristic of past effective administrators is now but rarely a component of any successful president's or dean's style.

The sociological conditions that prompted these changes are many and range from the improved access to colleges and universities to the expansion of collaborative efforts between government, business, and higher education. But the point central to a discussion of the governance of universities and the management of conflict is that a contemporary administrator's decision making is not limited to discovering the true and the beautiful in the solitude of his or her study or in tête-à-têtes with a few confidantes—though both solitary meditation and inner-circle examination of complex issues are essential. It is as if universities had been gradually transformed from exclusive boutiques, to which one might be invited to sip tea while viewing the collections of designers whose taste was far more refined than one's own, to shops whose wares extend onto the sidewalk and where passersby finger the merchandise and occasionally resent having to take half-circle detours to avoid bumping into the stalls. No one should be surprised that nearly everyone has an opinion as to the quality of the stock—and that nearly everyone expresses it. Management/ leadership under such conditions is a hurly-burly, high-energy enterprise.

Only the naive are stunned when hit by certain premises and only the self-indulgent are bruised when they strike their shins against them: faculty salaries will never be high enough for the faculty and will always be too high for the legislature; concerts will never be loud enough for the students and will always be too loud for the neighbors; ball games will never be high-scoring enough to satisfy the alumni and always far too high-scoring to eliminate the mistrust of poets and philosophers; the liberal arts will never be respected enough to cheer the department of foreign languages and will always be too respected to suit the local tool and dye shops; end of term parties will never be free-spirited enough to calm those who have taken final examinations and always too free-spirited to please the members of the board of trustees whose memories of tests are as faded as the snapshots of their own collegiate days. Rain does fall on picnics and someone out there somewhere has *not* been consulted.

An administrator who allows such postulates to drive him or her to any but short, aberrant moments of self-pity and discouragement is simply unsuited for the life of a president, vice-president or dean in a modern college or university. The morning mail will often include letters of advice and complaints and, upon occasion, even colorful threats. And if an issue has ignited a brush fire here and there, one letter will make clear that good judgment calls for your deciding matters one way while another letter will point out that common sense alone would suggest that the opposite is most certainly true and perhaps even beautiful. Many a letter or memo writer thinks it effective to map out the dire consequences not only for the institution, but for the career of the decision maker who should take care not to make the wrong move in a chess game that is always the most important of the decade. Other epistolary artists confine themselves to suggesting that all eyes are upon the hand about to move the queen, for a master is what this university needs and, quite frankly, some have noted signs of amateurishness. The author of the missive is, of course, not among those who have been so perceptive and, indeed, finds it painful even to put the assessment into words.

There is no denying that some days bring with them strong winds. And one needs to remain young and supple enough in spirit to be able to bend now this way, now that way, while at the same time firm and strong enough never to be uprooted. Barring the rare but not unknown conflicts that leave nothing but devastation in their wake, senior administrators everywhere are able to withstand strong buffeting from all directions without being torn asunder because they understand, respect, and observe certain principles of authenticity, responsibility, and compassion/detachment.

Authenticity

The authentic voice is perhaps the single strongest unifying element an administrator is able to offer an institution. An authentic voice transcends style, personal ambitions, and fears. An authentic voice frames visions and strobe-lights dreams. An administrator with an authentic voice neither exaggerates nor minimizes what an institution is and what it can become. Such an administrator does not speak one way to those who wear pin-stripe suits, another way to those who don tweeds, and yet a third way to those who favor blue jeans. Such an administrator does not even modify his or her diction, for such a person knows who he or she is, understands the intimate relationship between language and personality, and, knowing full well how easily one can become the person one pretends to be, has no interest in the use of masks.

The more complex the times, the faster the speed of change and the more everyone needs and values the well-lit stage of authenticity. Those who have attached themselves to colleges and universities as principal players, bit players, understudies, or simply spectators are no exception. A careful cultivation of authenticity extends far beyond simple truth telling—though it includes it, of course. It involves a total dedication to quality control: an examination of every decision for consistency with values that have been enunciated; an insistence that diplomacy and politics not become euphemisms for deceit; a profound faith that certain traditional convictions of the academy (e.g., that to know is better than not to know; that openness is preferred to secrecy; that academic freedom must be cherished, etc.) are not the subjects of compromise.

However, administrators will arrive on a campus with pockets filled not only with the traditional convictions that form the core of the academic culture, but bulging with smaller shells that they have picked up along the shore as they considered the wisdom of this view versus that one, as they dreamed this dream and not the other. The manner of choosing and defending these exceedingly important but second-tier concerns over which disputes are waged will distinguish one leader from another and will often test a leader's authenticity.

Let us, for example, imagine the case of a president newly appointed to a comprehensive university where faculty are bitterly divided over the appropriateness of highlighting scholarship in the reward system. Since this debate had already caused serious rancor in nearly all departments before the president's appointment, he had been asked his views on the matter during his interviews as candidate and he had, so he thought, been both thorough and forthright in expressing them. However, highly emotional contexts often make for poor acoustical settings and, in this case, both camps had found complex reasons to hope.

Within months of his accepting the presidency of this university, shortly before the rank committees meet to arrive at tenure and promotion recommendations, the president is asked by the academic senate to make clear in writing the degree of importance he attaches to research in a comprehensive university that offers baccalaureate and master's degrees. He repeats what he had said when he was interviewed and when he had met in informal sessions with the deans and the chairs of departments earlier in the term.

It is not his intent to reward scholars who do not take teaching seriously nor to reward teachers who do not take their scholarship seriously. He is convinced that the sine qua non of teaching excellence is knowledge of the discipline being taught—including the work of those pushing its frontiers. He is further persuaded that while stimulating and demanding teaching in the classroom is the most important evidence of accomplishment as a teacher, teaching in a university is not limited to the instruction of those who register for courses. Dedicated teaching extends itself to sharing knowledge with colleagues interested in particular disciplines. He insists that scholarship in this case is appropriately defined broadly enough to include the application, dissemination, and interpretation of new knowledge as well as the discovery of new knowledge. His important point is that a faculty member's teaching should not be fenced in by the borders of his or her classroom or laboratory. In short, according to this president, excellence in teaching depends in great part on excellence in scholarship; the two are separated only at the peril of one or the other. And he has no intention of emphasizing one at the expense of the other.

Both camps are disappointed, for a tie is to a complex emotional issue what jello is to dinner: an unsatisfactory ending. However, the authenticity of an administrator's convictions are not measured by the satisfaction they give his or her constituents. Indeed, their authenticity is diminished in proportion to the adjustments made to them for the sole purpose of pleasing some individual or group. Hence, the president holds firm.

Now, let us further imagine that in this instance the members of the camp who oppose any emphasis placed on scholarship in the reward system decide to see just how much displeasure our newly appointed president, with his polished convictions, can bench press. Within days of his mailing the requested written statement to the faculty, he receives a letter signed by some five or six senior professors that in essence distorts, with malice and sarcasm afore-thought, his judgments on the place of scholarship in that type of an institution.

These five or six faculty assure the president that his message has been received and taken to heart. Already they have planned to change their days and ways. In order to work on papers that will advance their disciplines they will no longer lose time volunteering to sit on committees and they will no longer spend more than the absolutely required minimum time in their offices for the purpose of advising students. Furthermore, since the grading of essay examinations is time consuming and carries no reward or recognition from the administration, they will henceforth confine their efforts to examinations that can be assessed by machines. Additional adolescent spleen covers three lamentable pages, and the president must be tempted to indulge in further explanations that would eventually risk diluting the purity of his convictions—convictions that are both sincere and thoughtful. For if they are not truthful and have not been considered seriously, they should never have been uttered to begin with. Since they have been, they must now be preserved whole at whatever cost. To do otherwise would be to engage in politics of the most egregious and unbecoming sort.

The depth of every administrator's convictions will be sounded; the likelihood of his or her providing effective leadership will be diminished to the degree that any constituency discovers them to be shallow. An authentic voice will not please everyone, but an authentic voice will reach everyone, even those in the far corners of the balcony, and an authentic voice will draw the respect and support of those who are sincerely interested in the long-term welfare of a college or university as opposed to its short-term peace.

Responsibility

Many senior administrators have had to adjudicate the claims and counterclaims of the advocates and opponents of faculty and classified employee unions; of proponents of minority rights; of supporters of animal rights; of representatives of national, regional, and local agencies; and of activists for many serious causes that fire the imagination of the caring under certain political conditions. They have learned for life that few ever proffer advice that is totally without merit. The need to study the relative merit of often contradictory advice is often described as overwhelming by those who must balance the many constituencies that may appear to enjoy perpetual conflict and may seem to have banished reason into exile.

Administrative control is not a popular phrase in the lexicon of the academy; it lacks the cachet of phrases like shared governance and academic freedom. However, when conflict erupts, administrative control—not in the sense of administrative domination but in the sense of administrative composure, self-confidence, and courage—ultimately plays as important a part in the protection of the traditional values of openness on a campus as do shared governance and academic freedom. The alternative to administrative control is not faculty/student/community control, but no control. Without it the center simply will not hold. In times of dissension, the last thing an institution needs is administrators who are torn by a need to please everyone. And the next to last thing it needs is administrators who cannot make decisions that will not muster popular support. All reasonable persons understand these truisms; they view administrators who seem not to understand them with impatience, even with contempt.

Hence, an administrator not only listens, but truly hears; then, after acknowledging the degree of merit in all arguments, an administrator unapologetically and unequivocally makes a decision and explains it. This is not an act of arrogance, but a refusal to cede decision making to those who do not bear the ultimate responsibility for the decision.

This is not an embracing of the banal conclusion that there is consolation in making one's own mistakes, but a calm recognition that a responsible administrator writes his or her own scripts.

Only the naive subscribe to the philosophy of a university president, not long for the administrative world, who claimed that "all persons of good will could come to agree if they talked long enough." Some want smoking banned on campus and some do not; some want fraternities outlawed and some do not; some want athletics promoted and some do not. One member of the state legislature will make clear that good judgment calls for the appointment of a particular individual and another member of the legislature will suggest that unpleasant consequences will follow the appointment of that same individual. One wealthy member of the alumni will give to the institution only if a student/faculty exchange is established with mainland China and another equally wealthy graduate, who spent years in Taiwan, will give to the institution only if the mainland Chinese are never invited to campus. If a bullying member of the state legislature, a potential donor, an irascible faculty committee, an irresponsible student newspaper editor, or a threatening member of the alumni is allowed to write one line of the administrator's script dealing with conflicts, to make one ultimate decision on one stage direction, the administrator has lost control. And an administrator who has lost control is the only administrator likely to be torn asunder by warring constituencies.

Compassion/Detachment

Henry James believed that in order to be a good novelist one had to be a good human being. Without fussing with the metaphysics of *good*, what appears to be true for the novelist is true for the administrator if, as is the case in James, one includes in the characterization of a good person the ability to enter imaginatively into another's world of pain and to care about it without losing one's way in it. Hence, in this

sense, good administrators never seek revenge against constituents who wish that they were exercising their authenticity and their control somewhere else or, worse, who accuse
the administrators of being devoid of one or the other or
both. Administrators must encourage in all constituents
their genuine responses; they must consider all but the frivolous ones seriously. However, compassion must not persuade administrators to abandon a detachment that protects
them from making unwise, unwarranted, or sentimental
moves. To respond imaginatively and sympathetically to *ad
misericordiam* arguments is to exercise compassion; to respond uncritically and illogically to *ad misericordiam* arguments is to fail to exercise detachment. Compassion and detachment are not mutually exclusive, but there is no denying
that rowing with these two oars makes for demanding and
skillful crossings.

Authenticity, control, compassion and detachment will
not, of course, bring all foxes to bay. Many will disapprove
of this or that; some will hold grudges; a few may even want
to take up a collection for a president's moving expenses.
After months of working with professional architects, amateur architects will tell you that you not only built the library in the wrong place, but that the entrance should have
faced west instead of east and that the circulation desk has
been finished with the wrong shade of oak stain. Linguists
will complain that in an otherwise brilliant speech, you misused the word *hagiographic*. Local haberdashers and their
spouses will blame you for messages on the t-shirts of members of fraternities, and fraternities will dismiss you as a geriatric prude. Politicians will become outraged over your low
and high admission standards. Students will condemn you
for belonging to an establishment that supports apartheid,
and board members will condemn you for sympathizing
with the students. Assessing the amount of time and the degree of seriousness one should properly assign to each of
these complaints and concerns is part of the art of decision
making. Constituents will simply pitch them at you; if you
flinch, you are out. A good administrator knows when to
duck them, when to foul them off so as to protect the plate,

and when to swing at them hard. That is the knowledge one can master; that is the knowledge that inspires trust.

In making administrative decisions, both large and small, it is useful to remember that matters of importance are not limited to questions of life, liberty, and the pursuit of happiness—or rather, that the pursuit of happiness might well include the shade of oak stain. In *The Untouchables*, the 1988 film version of the classic confrontation between the gangster, Al Capone, and the federal agent, Elliot Ness, one of Ness's fellow agents asks him how his wife fills her days while he dedicates himself nearly obsessively to investigating the activities of Capone. Ness answers that she is busy choosing decorative colors for their kitchen. With a naif's awe at the range of human possibility, he says something like the following, "Just imagine—in the midst of all this carnage and violence, somebody cares about the color of the kitchen." But that is precisely the point: one of the precious values of civilized conditions is that one is free to care about the color of kitchens and the shade of oak stain on library circulation desks.

Undoubtedly, upon rare occasions, a confluence of circumstances will produce a "Gilbert" with 200 mile-an-hour winds that level skillful management, honest appraisals, calm behavior, and wise leadership. However, while the winds of an administrator's days do change speed and direction, most are without the strength to inflict significant harm on those firmly bound to values appropriate to an academic culture.

OTHER VOICES, OTHER VIEWS

From the President of a Community College:

Few of us work in high consensus environments. The broader the scope of one's responsibilities, the greater the likelihood that we will be pressed with inconsistent demands. We're unlikely to eliminate the constituencies, so I believe it is very important to be clear about the extent to which you will meet the demands of different groups. The alternative is to do nothing or to equivocate about the extent to which you will meet demands. The former results in your being perceived as a weak leader and the latter as an unprincipled leader. You have to stand for something—even when it means saying no and making people unhappy.

From the President of a Private College:

An administrator is chosen to work with different constituencies; if he's torn by them, he doesn't understand the nature of his job. Besides, constituencies don't always have to be in conflict. When they are, the administrator must still work with them and try to bring about whatever resolution is appropriate at the time.

Most important for the administrator is to remember always the nature of each constituency, its relative importance to the issue at hand, and its part in the institutional power structure.

From the Vice-President for Academic Affairs at a Public University:

Academic types are by virtue of training (and on occasion—I presume genetic predisposition) cynical. Over the long haul, such cynicism (healthy skepticism) serves academe nicely by reinforcing a commitment to the search for truth. Over the short haul, academic cynicism creates within and between faculties and other collegiate constituencies considerable tension, argument, and debate. The net effect is to create an administrative experience (for this writer at least) which has been described to others, metaphorically, as similar to the experience of "herding cats."

Thus, I find this myth truthful and inevitable for those who venture into administration. In a very real sense, this thesis of inevitable conflict is part of the "not for the faint hearted" adage often quoted in discussions of administrative careers.

From the Dean of a Branch Campus at a Public University:

I have known some administrators who never have been "torn" by anything though they believed themselves to be on the ramparts for everything. Your public image as portrayed through newspaper accounts or television segments can be "torn up." You can be "torn down" by campus groups and outside groups (some of which are your constituencies) when argument, essential in a university, is contaminated by campus (and system) politics, by special pleading, and by the ideologue's masquerade.

I don't believe you are "torn by conflicting constituencies" when you thoughtfully and honestly arrive at the ground upon which you will stand. It can be unpleasant, distressing and disturbing, emotionally draining. You can, additionally, be "torn by" conflicting loyalties and conflicting personally held judgments.

From the Vice-President for Academic Affairs at a Private College:

After a recent evaluation report by a visiting accrediting team which commented on the "internal climate" of my institution, I was directed by a committee of the board of trustees to bring order to the ranks of the faculty, explain to them the wisdom of so doing, and achieve greater productivity from them in the process. On the same day I met with the trustee group, a collection of senior professors laid on my desk a directive that I urge the trustees to launch a new capital campaign directed specially at raising faculty salaries to a new high, reducing teaching loads by a third, and increasing the size of the faculty by a corresponding number.

I think I felt torn by conflicting constituencies that afternoon. Neither the board nor the faculty will get its way, and both groups will grimly suspect that I am somehow at the root of their disappointment.

From the President of a Private College:

While you stand there, tattered and bleeding, remember that if there were no conflicts, your job would be superfluous.

Managers and executives have to remember, in the back of their minds, that unless they are performing some key functions like selling the institution or settling conflicts about plans, operations, and evaluation of results, they are unnecessary overhead in the educational process.

Remember when you were a dean or faculty member (or even a middle manager fighting for departmental or divisional turf in business or government) how strong the forces were for you to stir up conflict and confrontation. Study some of the recent literature on decision making and conflict resolution, and for solace and more philosophical musings, dip back into history and literature for some of the case studies they provide. And stay philosophical: I can't quote him exactly, but Tip O'Neill—at a dinner which brought Washingtonians of all stripes together—commented to Gerry Ford: What a wonderful country this is, that we can come together at a session like this and say how genuinely we love and respect each other; and three months from now, in the campaign, you know I'll be touring the country kicking your ass!

From the Dean of Arts and Sciences at a Public University:

Some administrators avoid conflict at all cost or approach it in a very public way which invites exacerbation of the conflict, since no one likes to lose in a public forum. I have often assumed the role of the "loser" instead. Here is what I really do. When I find out that a conflict exists—between [the departments of] music and theater, for example, both of which units feel that the other is getting more performance resources and support than they deserve—I talk individually and privately with faculty members in their offices (not mine) to get a sense of the dimensions of the problem. They know, of course, that I am talking to others, but I never attribute any particular views to anyone. Then, assuming that I can infer a way out of the problem, I invite the constituencies to a meeting and offer a deliberately imperfect compromise proposal. To demonstrate its imperfections, I may even "plant" a couple of challenges to it, which usually has the effect of inviting other challenges and proposals for revision. Since I am now the one who is making adjustments and compromises, I am the one who is "losing" and the faculty members are discovering areas of agreement to which they would probably never admit. After eliciting all the corrections and revisions I can, I redraft the proposal. It may take two or three cycles of this process to resolve the conflict, but I as an individual am not "torn" by the process. The faculty love to instruct the administrators in the way things ought to work, and usually they find large areas of agreement and relatively small areas of disagreement.

From the Interim President of a Public University:

I suppose we have to keep in mind that half-truths are generally half true. So administrators may expect some mental anguish over trying to satisfy the often conflicting but legitimate needs of varying constituencies. But as with most aphorisms, the opposite is equally true. An administrator may, in fact, continue to have a future so long as his or her constituencies remain in conflict; when they gang up on him or her, however, he or she is through. The wisest and best of administrators will, of course, attempt to focus the energies aroused by conflict upon some indisputably common purpose and achievable goal. Resolving conflict or turning it to good purpose would seem to me one of the major responsibilities of any administrator. And there's some wear and tear in any job.

From the President of a Public University:

Administrators will certainly be called upon to preside over conflicting interests by various constituencies. Whether such necessity results in his or her being "torn" in an emotional sense probably varies. Few executive positions in our society hold responsibilities to such varied constituencies: students, faculty, several varieties of staff, parents, alumni, friends, donors, and public officials (for public institutions). The list is probably not complete. Obviously, these groups pursue differing interests which sometimes (usually?) conflict. It is one of the things which makes the job fun.

From the Vice-President for Academic Affairs at a Public University:

It is a truism that most administrators serve many constituencies and that those in central administration find pressures from the constituencies most challenging. In my opinion, the primary challenge is serving those constituencies fairly and well while remaining consistent with the mission of the institution and moving in appropriate instructional directions.

I find the word "torn" to be a loaded term. Whether or not an administrator is "torn" depends on his or her philosophy and practices. Personally, I feel responsive to the various needs, challenged by meeting them, and sometimes disappointed. I do not feel "torn."

From the Provost of a Public University:

The aphorism [myth] is overstated. My experience is that there is competition for scarce resources by different constituencies and there are differences of opinion on most issues. One expects controversy and approaches decisions by having full discussion, listening to all sides, and modifying proposed solutions to take into account the unique problems of all interested groups. Having made the decision, one should be prepared to explain the reasons for the decision.

If this approach is used, those who have been involved will usually regard the outcome as "fair" and are likely to understand the necessity for not meeting all of their needs. I have never felt "torn" or under constant fire because of these decisions.

From the President of a Public University:

Indeed, from time to time the interests of students, faculty, staff, trustees, alumni, legislators, and financial supporters may be at odds. However, most of the time the interests reflected by these constituencies are relatively compatible and do not place substantial strain on the administrator. When the administrator experiences strain or tear, it is most often a reflection of the fact that the administrator is guided by the principle of pleasing each of the constituencies rather than having guiding principles and values which he follows in the performance of his administrative role. Indeed, all administrators find themselves in situations where it is not possible to take action which will be universally applauded by all constituencies. Taking action which will from time to time displease a single group of constituents should not necessarily be a wrenching experience for an administrator.

From the Dean of a College of Arts and Sciences at a Public University:

Perhaps "torn" is too strong a word to use, but administrators must continually work with conflicting and shifting constituencies. Not to recognize that constituencies exist is a grave error. Compounding the problem is the failure to take into account that constituencies can dissolve and reform differently, depending on the issue. Administrators live in a "political" arena and must work with various constituencies. The trick is to arrive at viable solutions that are at least acceptable to the various constituencies. I would hope that an administrator is not identified with a particular constituency. This ensures that the administrator is not torn by conflicting constituencies but is viewed as a facilitator in arriving at viable solutions.

From the Vice-President for Academic Affairs at a Public University:

Very few constituencies enjoy long-term conflict and in most instances are interested in finding a resolution.

Chapter 8

An Administrator Will Be Lonely at the Top

In a recent study conducted by Dr. Marvel Williamson of the University of Iowa, as reported in *Administrator*, a management newsletter, presidents of universities carry out "73.28 activities during a typical day, each with a mean duration of 7.39 minutes." Consequently, "moments of solitude appear for about 5 minutes at a time" (*Administrator*, January 11, 1988, Vol. 7, no. 1). All but Aristotelians convinced that "only God or a wild beast can endure solitude" may be disconcerted if not shaken by such data. Indeed, some may find even the gathering of such information yet another depressing sign that we live in a place and time where numbers are encouraged to do more than they were ever intended to do.

However, though a president's infrequent moments of solitude lasting four, five, or six minutes may make for very dull conversation in any setting, this kind of stopwatch research does point to a matter of serious import: Have university CEOs and other administrators so defined, or allowed others to so define, the nature of their responsibilities that they lead unexamined lives of the mind? Have they, with ironic inertia, accepted a view of success that makes for days of jumping from one rolling river log to another and for nights of exhaustion along the shores?

For one of the central truths in the life of a university administrator is this: hours of solitude necessary for the wise, thoughtful, and well-planned leadership of an institution are obtained only as a result of a self-discipline and a self-confidence undeterred by the criticism of the many who would take "but a minute of your time."

If by characterizing as lonely the professional life of a senior-level administrator, especially that of a president, one intends to suggest days unfrequented by people, then it is most certainly *not* lonely at the top. It is, on the contrary, noisy and crowded and hot at the top. A president and other senior administrators are pulled, pushed, and upon occasion, unceremoniously shoved, but administrators are never ignored. And thereby hangs the challenge, for intelligent leadership is conceived in solitude. It is but rarely formulated at conferences, seminars, and symposia, however useful; nor at gatherings ironically called *retreats*, as if "retreating" were not a matter of seclusion and solitude. The wise course of action, the appropriate phrasing of a decision, the compassionate and humane way to behave are discovered, if not in deserts and on mountain tops, in offices when all but the security officers have gone, in studies far from the madding crowd.

In *Kafka's Other Trial*, Elias Canetti (Schocken, New York, 1969, p. 37) quotes from one of Franz Kafka's letters to his fiancee, Felice Bauer.

> You once said you would like to sit beside me while I write. Listen, in that case I could not write. . . . For writing means revealing oneself to excess. . . . This is why one can never be alone enough when one writes, why there can never be enough silence around one when one writes, why even night is not night enough.

Neither university presidents nor anyone else who has accepted the responsibilities of leadership will refine a vision or a voice in the spotlights and cacophony of days crammed with an uncritical and resigned acceptance of meetings, receptions, electronic messages, mail, and telephone calls; with a sitting on innumerable boards, with a ceremonial greeting of every group of guests, and a welcoming of anyone who wants to eat a madeleine on someone else's time.

However, two temptations constantly seek lodging in an Administrator's office:

One, accessibility and good will mean more in the long run than study and close consideration of issues. It is very difficult to resist a temptation that leads to a daily sense of accomplishment. And it is especially difficult when remaining on the surface of days is considerably less demanding than donning diving gear and exploring the depths. In some echo chamber of the mind, one hears a tinny defensive voice: I *did* put in a good day. I met with the directors of the chamber of commerce; I raised another sizable scholarship from the alumni; I found a solution to the dispute between two vice-presidents; I wrote ten memos; I returned fifteen telephone calls. I have had an impact after one or two or three years of such giving of self. Why, I received over 600 Christmas cards this year. True, some were from the Watson Asbestos Removal Company and Armstrong's Floral Arrangements for All Occasions—but still . . .

Two, the vision and the voice brought to an administrative post were honed through years of experience and need no further examination or change. Falling into this temptation may lead to even more serious consequences than falling into the first, for a frequent reexamination of premises in the changing light of new knowledge and new perspectives forms not only a portion of the core of higher education's mission, but a segment of its commonly accepted culture. At one time of the year or another, in one assembly or another, everyone in the academy talks of life-long learning, of bringing in consultants for fresh insights, of reappraising this or that portion of the curriculum or this or that policy, and it spends millions in search of new wisdom at gatherings in Washington Hiltons and San Francisco Sheratons. The serious re-read Plato, Montaigne, and Proust, not only to take unto themselves their wisdom but to understand more fully their errors. It would, therefore, be ironic indeed if the many lives of an academic administrator did not include the life of truly open and detached continual inquiry.

To resist falling into these two temptations and to help her associates do the same, one president sets aside a portion of every week, however busy, for the purpose of study. She schedules it into the calendar. She also asks the vice-presidents who report to her to do the same—very much in the manner in which she asked the deans to do so during her tenure as a provost. And by *study* she does not mean a reading of the popular magazine of higher education; she means further reading in those disciplines about which she and her colleagues may already know something and background reading in those disciplines where they might be less secure. Quite simply, she asks herself and other administrators to lead lives of the mind that are in keeping with the ideals espoused in classrooms, convocations, and commencements. Ultimately, these are solitary voyages; there are no group tours to the land of intellectual insight and wisdom—though we may with profit view one another's slides upon our return. Hence, an academic administrator must first seek and then keep periods of solitude. And this solitude is as far removed from the dejection associated with loneliness as hope is from despair.

But perhaps those who find meaning in this myth intend something quite different. Perhaps the loneliness they find at the top is unattached to notions of dejection and desolation by virtue of solitude. Undoubtedly, when referring to this myth some point to the distance between themselves and others exacted by the responsibilities of office. With funereal tone, the clichés mount: "The buck stops here." "I'm the one who has to fish or cut bait." "The tough decisions are mine and mine alone." "I bear full responsibility for the actions taken by my staff." This last brave dictum is usually spoken with a catch in the throat.

While there is, of course, a sense in which the head of a division and the head of a university are responsible for all deeds, praiseworthy and condemnable, within the unit or the institution they administer, there is also a sense in which this academic world view is unadulterated heroics. Others have crossed mountains and forests in wagons, braved white whales with harpoons, mastered the Mississippi by raft, maintained innocence in a corrupt Europe. Contemporary managers are left with press conferences at which they accept responsibility for the significant increase in enrollments and the rise in an entering class's SAT verbal scores; at which they accept responsibility for the bursar's absconding with the library funds or the librarian's absconding with the bursar's wife. To be managerially accountable is not, however, always to be ethically accountable and the distinction should be maintained. No president, vice-president, or dean is singlehandedly the source of the good and the evil sufficient unto the day thereof. And to contribute to a fiction that imagines it otherwise is to feed others pabulum.

The tone of the writing of some observers of higher education portray a university president as one who never totally reveals himself or herself to a staff who are supposedly kept in awe of this charismatic leader and deliberately kept off balance by the unpredictability of his or her brilliant moves. Such depictions suggest that the writers may have seen too many Westerns in their impressionable years. Hopalong Cassidy, Gene Autry, and even Roy Rogers never said much about who stole the cattle until they were ready to run some thieves out of town, but they would have had to have confided in a gabby Gabby Hayes or to have sought counsel from an uninspired Andy Devine.

The deans who now sit on a provost's council or the vice-presidents who now form a president's staff are not foils designed to set off the heroic dimensions of one who caps off flow charts. Contemporary leaders of colleges and universities need not die alone on the prairie any more than they need to narrow their eyes when circumstances force them to think. The academic world is peopled with talented deans and vice-presidents who are discreet and loyal and wise and who can be trusted to discuss the details of any problem, any challenge, any fear, and any dream. A senior-level administrator who is professionally lonely in decision making either inherited a weak staff or appointed a weak staff or clung too long to the heroic image of a leader as one who stands in solitary distance and wisdom from companions who find joy and reward in the undignified role of sidekicks.

A few years back, two issues of the *New Yorker* ran a profile of Andre Previn as conductor, and the author reported that when asked whether he trusted his orchestra players, Previn replied that not only did he trust them, but that one of the best bits of advice he ever received came from his principal horn player in the London Symphony: "Andre, when you get lost in a piece—and you will—make nice, vague motions for a while, and we'll sort it out for you. But if you start flogging away at us, we're all lost" (*New Yorker*, January, 1983, p. 56). The anecdote is an amusing and appropriate metaphor for university administration, where regardless of the job description filed in personnel offices, the responsibilities always converge on persuading hundreds of highly educated, often very talented individualists to agree to play the same work with roughly the same interpretation and in harmony. And Previn is right: the more complex the piece, the more chances there are of desperate mistakes, the less wise it is to flail one's arms as if by doing so one could extract rich tones from the violin section. One should trust the very accomplished players. And in administration as in life, trust begets trust, loyalty begets loyalty.

While senior administrators cannot demand richness of tone from any section of the academic orchestra, they can and should conduct affairs in such a way that richness of tone is inspired, fostered, and rewarded. And success in conducting of this kind requires creating conditions that make professional loneliness and disengagement, if not impossible, at least highly unlikely both for the administrators and for all members of their immediate administrative teams.

The means are at hand: one cultivates a sense of common cause; one cultivates a sense of perspective.

A university president, whose character was fired for six years in the hot kiln of a New England boarding school, cherishes the following anecdote. One fall, the headmistress of this ascetic school foraged for additional motivating spurs with which to inspire others to, as she put it, "be larger than themselves." While thus occupied, she came upon the notion of organizing her charges into two camps that would henceforth compete in everything from mastering geometric theorems to scoring field hockey goals. The idea, one gathered, was to transcend the self; to find, as Henry James might have put it, "absorbing errands." The headmistress, in whose breast Jesus and Nietzsche arm wrestled, titled her two camps *Serviam* (I serve) and *Ducam* (I lead). In a rare attempt at shared governance, an attempt she soon came to regret, she allowed the students to inscribe their names under the banner of their choice. In attractive innocence and honesty, some 95% of the young women signed their names under the heading *Ducam*. Undaunted, the headmistress returned shared governance to the back of the closet, reminded one and all that the meek would inherit the earth, and arbitrarily divided the student body into two equal parts. But for reasons that puzzled her, no one's heart was ever engaged. After one year of lackluster contests, the banners disappeared and the students were left with two Latin words and a small parable for their own archives.

Every academic president, vice-president and dean would have joined the *Ducam* camp; to ignore that realization is certainly unwise, and perhaps even dangerous. The contemporary popular rhetoric of *service* is far removed from concepts of servility or humility or subservience or meekness. Administrators talk of wanting to serve the university, the community, and the nation in the same sense as political candidates to the Unites States Senate talk of serving their constituents: in both cases service is a euphemism of choice for leadership; in both cases service is a code of understanding for leadership. Successful administrators know that such universally accepted manners of speech are not simply rhetorical devices, but are cherished symbols within an academic culture of the belief in and even the need for shared leadership.

Hence, the most appropriate and effective tone for the advancement of a university is one that militates against loneliness at the top. It is a tone that if honest and properly modulated rarely needs to remind anyone as to where the last word lies. On the other hand, it does remind everyone that the cause is a common one; it is, therefore, imperative that all who care reason together to reach conclusions that are most often out of the realm of right or wrong and into the far more complex realm of wise and unwise. It is a tone that leads to the joys of shared victories and the consolations of shared defeats. The culture of academic administration is a "we culture" as apposed to an "I culture."

This view does not suggest that a president yields the floor to the voice of the ballot box. For example, one president, who by the end of the first year in office was half-way through rebuilding a very weak president's staff, found himself in a danger zone. The time had come to appoint a dean to one of the university's large and influential colleges. While recommending three candidates, the search committee made clear its unanimous conviction that candidate one, the only insider, outdistanced all others. Candidate one had spent the entire year tirelessly running for the position in ways that left the president convinced that he possessed neither the qualities of mind or heart that were needed to lead a strong and demanding faculty. The provost, whose resignation had already been requested, was not inclined to take a dangerous high road; the faculty who had been promised a land of milk and honey by candidate one wrote eloquent, sincere, and nearly persuasive letters of support. Meanwhile, the president concluded that candidate three was the person whose values and style the college and university needed at this moment in its history.

The president was understandably apprehensive, but not alone. He had already hired two vice-presidents and an executive assistant who were experienced and trustworthy. Worries were shared; consequences were anticipated; strategies of honest communication were planned. And the college watched. The president, who was not for a moment alone, strapped himself to the mast and appointed candidate three. The storm passed—as most storms do—and an administrative team was solidified. With but few exceptions, the faculty understood that their views had been seriously considered

and respected, but that a president had to have the courage
of his or her judgments. It helped that candidate three
turned out to be a splendid dean! But the point meant for
emphasis here is that experiences such as these, the very
warp and woof of administrative life, should be used to
strengthen an exhilarating sense of common cause.

The common cause will remain exhilarating in part to
the extent that a senior administration maintains perspective. Presidents who cannot step outside themselves long
enough to see the humorous, as opposed to the heroic, figure
they cut—strapped to the mast while waves batter them—
are perhaps the ones given to loneliness at the top. Many
a serious event on campuses is simultaneously a humorous
event. A ten-page letter from Professor X forecasting the approach of Armageddon because Professor Y has been chosen
to be honored at commencement is both serious and comical. An alumnus who calls to announce that he will withdraw his pledge of a large sum to help build the concert hall
because he witnessed students displaying what he termed
obscene placards is both serious and comical. An editorial in
the college daily that distorts beyond all recognition your
carefully crafted fall address to the assembled faculties is
both serious and comical. Your boarding a plane to give a
talk to a group of important colleagues across the country
and discovering over Chicago that you hold a folder containing the address you gave to the local chamber of commerce
is both serious and comical. Administrators who fail to hold
these contradictions in mind with some degree of grace and
poise are administrators whose sense of their own grandeur
and that of their own ambitions is apt to create moats that
few staff members will find it worthwhile to cross. Genuine
crises are rare. One vice-president who confessed to feeling
dejected and alone in decision making was one who had
never been able to build a unified staff, for she unconsciously
welcomed the excitement of crises. For this woman, a day
without a crisis was a crisis. Conflicts gave zest to her days
and a drought of them led her to choreograph elaborate rain
dances and to describe the resulting showers as floods. Only

the newly appointed or the duty bound returned her calls.

One wonders if this lack of humor that continues to contribute to the myth of loneliness at the top is not ironically strengthened by the sentimentality that has attached itself to the concept of mentoring "like a tin can to a dog's tail"— to borrow from Yeats. Since teaching in all its multiple forms has always been of serious concern in the academy, all those who have spent years in university administration have, of course, both received and given guidance. However, the method and consequences of so doing in the not-distant past seemed less self-conscious, less studied, less noisy than it has become in the last few years. Much of the present-day talk and writing surrounding the rituals of mentoring are harmlessly pretentious when not downright silly. But what may be less innocent are the contributions that this handbook mentality have made to views of senior administrators as solitary figures of power who may bestow, and conversely, withdraw attention and support; as opposed to senior administrators as colleagues with whom one differs and works and dreams. The inflated value of attaining mentors that has spread across the administrative land has less to do with a discovered passion for learning than an unseemly passion for power. The adoring gaze and the pasted smile should remain, if remain they must, the purgatorial province of the politician's mate. Senior academic administrators who invite and reward adoration, a state foreign to a culture that encourages query and debate and criticism, are the ones most apt to discover themselves alone at the top.

A good administrative team is not a family, but it does share two characteristics with a good family. One, it keeps all its members directed toward a common cause and prevents any of its members from transforming the trivial into the serious. And, two, in the words of John Updike, it "teaches us how love exists in a realm beyond liking or disliking, co-existing with indifference, rivalry, and even antipathy" ("Brother Grasshopper," *New Yorker*, December 14, 1987, p. 46.). And where one loves, one is never alone.

OTHER VOICES, OTHER VIEWS

[We were in this instance especially eager to hear from presidents, but did include the views of those who were one or two breaths away when confronting this myth]

From the President of a Private College:

Several years ago when I first became a dean, the wife of an Army officer remarked to me, "From now on you will never know who your friends are." Since I considered myself a friendly, gregarious type, and since I was being made dean at an institution where I had long taught and where I was, I believed, surrounded by friends, I was skeptical.

Today, though I am still not completely convinced that it's altogether lonely at the top, I'm no longer as skeptical. The top is the top, the seat of what is believed to be, erroneously or not, the ultimate seat of power, and for whoever occupies it the realization must come that as boss he exists alone and without peers and that former friends are now first of all employees. As Shakespeare portrays it, one day Falstaff is a drinking buddy of Prince Hal in a local tavern; the next day Hal is King and Falstaff, now a mere subject, goes unacknowledged in a crowd of onlookers as the royal procession passes. One simply cannot have it both ways.

From the President of a Private College:

In one sense this myth is very true—one person carries ultimate responsibility for all decisions. It is amazing to me how much credit is attributed to the president for positive changes or results and, conversely, how much blame rests on that office when things aren't so great!

If one believes in and practices a "team approach" to administration, the loneliness is significantly reduced.

From the Acting President of a Public College:

No academic administrator lacks a corps of colleagues, each of whom believes him- or herself to be eminently more qualified than the administrator to make decisions and establish policy for the institution. Clearly, the higher the administrative position, the more distance one places between oneself and this army. When I consider my closest advisors, the individuals upon whom I rely for information and from whom I seek counsel, the number has actually increased a bit as I moved through appointments as dean, vice-president and acting president. As the identity of my advisors and confidants has changed, so has the balance of off- and on-campus members. The composition of my advisory group reflects the more global nature of the issues I must address, with presidential colleagues, corporate friends, and individuals in the political arena joining a more select group of individuals from the campus.

It does not have to be lonely at the top, but it is highly likely that one will have placed some distance between him- or herself and the campus community. The opportunity to be solely responsible for making important decisions about an institution, to leave one's mark on it, is a rare privilege which each of us has sought for the better part of a long career. We shouldn't denigrate the opportunity by wailing about a "lack of support."

From the President of a Private College:

I came up through the faculty ranks and after twenty years with many of my friends in the faculty, I did find it lonely at first. Administrative colleagues help make up for this, as well as other presidents—largely women. I talk often with other presidents on the phone, and that helps a great deal.

I'd like to comment—for what it's worth—that a single woman as president may find life lonelier than most since trustees do not include them in social gatherings with the ease and frequency that they include male presidents and their wives. I don't know whether the key here is sex, singleness, or the inability to play golf, but I know I'm not the only woman president to have this experience. As you might expect, female trustees are better in this regard than males.

I think loneliness is one of the reasons many presidents

spend time at national meetings. They won't learn much they don't know (or they shouldn't), but they will get a chance to see friends from presidential ranks all across the country and sharing stuff is helpful.

From the President of a Community College:

This [myth] has much to do with our societal perceptions of power and authority. Individuals sense that you, "at the top," have the capacity to affect their lives in some way and they protect themselves with distance and what they consider proper professional behavior. Oh for the staff member who has the confidence and comfort to say, "Boss, you're wrong!"

The isolation is mainly psychological. People believe that they are endangered if they fail to get along with you; they do not want to be on the other side of your decisions; they (mistakenly, I think) assume that you value acquiescence more than honesty. People are also ambivalent about your successes and do not want to be involved in your failures. They behave accordingly. The challenge is to build relationships in spite of these fears. It takes a strong sense of self to be a truly effective executive.

From the President of a Private College:

If you have been a dean and have had the camaraderie within a campus or across campuses of conniving with fellow deans to outwit central administration, it is an adjustment to find that within campus, you are indeed alone (unless as president in a multi-campus system, you can play the dean's role vis-à-vis a chancellor); across campuses, you are too fully booked with your major constituents and too competitive in the pitch for fund raising to have the time or reasons for coming together with other presidents.

Remedies (so that the entire load does not fall on a spouse or one or two tolerant friends):

1. Making sure that the board (or the next level up in a multi-campus system) provides some openings for informal

conversation and review as well as formal occasions for doing business.

2. Organizing, as a group of us business deans once did, a semi-annual weekend retreat of heads of non-competitive schools to work through a structured but informal agenda of ideas and issues that emerged from our experiences.

3. Remembering that time and energy should be reserved for one or two purely personal pursuits that have no other value than escape from the cocoon—community work, sailing, tennis, bird watching, whatever.

From the President of a Private College:

One cannot and should not become close friends with fellow senior officers or with members of the board of trustees, but one can and should be on friendly terms with these people and others associated with our institutions. Hence, it is *not* lonely at the top *except* briefly when one makes an unpopular, but necessary, decision, or if the senior officer group is *not* working as a team. One's counterparts at other colleges and universities or CEOs in the corporate world provide the necessary "pills" we need to take for maintaining patience or for regaining a sense of humor about what we see transpiring around us. Visits with counterparts at annual meetings and service on corporate boards keep me from being lonely at the top.

From the President of a Public University:

At each step a "layering" does occur, an isolation from those with whom I had earlier associated personally and professionally. . . . I miss the camaraderie of my colleagues, the casual chats over coffee, and the evenings and weekends when I could on the spur of the moment invite friends over for coffee or a cocktail. But I knew when I accepted the responsibilities of an administrator that I would be faced with making decisions which might alienate or anger some of those whose friendship and counsel I valued. When I made that conscious decision to become an administrator, I had to accept the reality that my personal and professional relationships would change.

I would advise those who aspire to administrative roles in higher education to do some soul searching before making the decision to accept such a role. If those persons think that their personal, social, or professional lives will continue in the same way as they had in the past, then perhaps some rethinking is in order.

While it is often lonely at the top, or put in front where you are the most visible—it is also true that the view is often the clearest and the best.

From the Provost of a Public University:

The statement [myth] is largely false. The higher we go "up the ladder" of professional achievement, the more we depend on others' good performance, good will, and loyalty. A manager who is not willing to let others grow by taking more and more responsibility for the organization and who is unable, for whatever reason, to win their loyalty may find himself or herself "lonely at the top," but not for very long!

From the Vice-Chancellor for Academic Affairs at a Public University:

It is my experience that it is indeed "lonely at the top." Why? Because (1) all "friendships" are based on the social necessity of entertaining and gratifying the egos of prospective donors, university "family" members, or supporters. And those who entertain chancellors and other administrators do so, not out of a natural affinity with peers, but solely out of duty. (2) Those who seem to share interests and offer their "friendship" rarely do so out of pure motives. One never knows when a dinner party, tennis match, or concert will turn into a lobbying effort on a particular issue. (3) One cannot trust the advice of most on campus. Their motives in offering a particular course of action are generally tainted with a desire to protect a particular interest of their own and sometimes even act out of pure perversity. (4) Finally, although organizations want strong leadership they generally resent it when it is provided. One feels, therefore, very much as though one must find an inner strength and close family/spousal support to survive.

From the Vice-Chancellor of a Public University:

The myth is that there is a top. As for lonely, there is seldom enough loneliness.

From the Dean of a Public College:

Actually, it's lonely as a faculty member. I taught for 12 years full-time before becoming an administrator, and in all that time I had exactly one ongoing group experience, a woman's study group that met each month on one Sunday, over two years or so, to read the new literature on women and to plan a women's studies program. (Department meetings don't really count.)

In ____ I became an assistant to the president. All of a sudden I had a "work family": the four other principal administrators, the other two presidential assistants, and various other co-workers. I loved it.

Since that enlightenment, I have gone on to two academic dean's positions. In each case, I again have a work family, with people to mentor, teams to work with, and things to get done. In this sense it is not lonely at the top or near the top. However, one still does have to take responsibility. Groups can make decisions or make recommendations, but they are not well suited for carrying them out or taking the blame. (They *can* take the credit). In that sense it's lonely.

From the Vice-Chancellor of a Public University:

It certainly isn't "lonely" at the top (if one means involvement in the human drama). It is, however, exploitative, shallow and superficial.

From the Vice-President for Academic Affairs of a Public University:

One of the most surprising things that occurred when I was appointed vice-president was the loss of campus colleague-ship. Suddenly, there's no one whom I can treat as a peer. The other campus vice-presidents are competitors for re-sources, turf, and policy leadership. When you are a dean, there are other deans with whom you can commiserate and discuss issues. If you are department chairperson, there is a wide range of colleagues with whom you can consult and share experiences. The vice-president for academic affairs inevitably has to go off campus to find colleagueship. So, indeed, from this perspective the position is lonely and I sus-pect the presidency is even lonelier.

The loneliness from the lack of colleagues is reinforced by a need to keep one's cards close to one's chest. Informal conversation and idle chitchat have to be carefully watched. This produces a social isolation that is troubling to many. However, it is not uncrowded at the top. The other striking thing that I've observed is how crowded the agenda and the calendar are. So if loneliness means being alone, it just ain't so. I have little time for myself, for reflection, or room for action. Everybody wants to talk to you, to get a moment, ask a question, or make a point. It's like administering in a crowded room in a busy hotel during the cocktail reception. But that's OK, I enjoy the hustle and bustle of leading a large organization. If I didn't, I should get out of the job.

From the Vice-President for Academic Affairs at a Public University:

I think there is some truth to this myth. People at the top management level are generally surrounded by advisors; ad-visors do just that—advise. They are not ultimately respon-sible for a decision and do not necessarily have to suffer from the consequences of bad decisions resulting from bad advice. Therefore, perspectives of the advisors are often different from that of the decision maker. Second, in too many instances the top level associates are also competitors for the top-level job, and many of them by their imagination or dream want to be in the same position of power as the person at the top.

From the Provost and Vice-President for Academic Affairs at a Public University:

Urban sociologists sometimes typify people's orientations to their lives as being "localite or cosmopolitan." A localite draws his or her friends, norms, values, and sense of self primarily with regard to others who reside in geographic proximity. The cosmopolitan, conversely, draws his or her sense of self in the main from a much more geographically diverse group. "Localites" tend to be much more attuned to events which reflect a closely bounded community of interest where cosmopolitans may find little to which to attend. Cosmopolitans are more likely to be affected by trends and events which have implications for their diffuse network—events which may be unrecognized by localites.

I suspect that whether it is "lonely at the top" depends to a great extent on the incumbent's and the institutional culture's positions with regard to this typology. From observing academic vice-presidents over the last six years, I would posit that when both the institution and the vice-president match in orientation, there is much greater likelihood that the vice-president will be accepted as a colleague and that the role will be less "lonely." Conversely, where the institutional cultures and the vice-president's life orientation are opposed, there will be little socio-emotional support from within the institution.

Epilogue

Few outgrow the need for stories. Nearly everyone reads them, tells them, embellishes them, denies them, creates them. Indeed, to understand an old person's compulsion to reminisce is to understand the never-diminishing urge to invent and re-invent structures for our days and ways and to describe and re-describe the texture of our visions and of our dreams. Popular myths for administrators, received ideas, are shared stories that attempt to impose some order and some meaning on professional lives spent in a slightly anarchical academic world. And the stories are told over and over again in an attempt to get them right: to place a precise degree of emphasis on one element as opposed to another, to eliminate one detail in favor of another, to highlight one insight instead of another.

But forever the story remains unfinished. Do administrators experience a honeymoon period? Some believe they do, and so, perhaps, they do. Are administrators lonely at the top? Some are and some are not. How does one define "lonely"? Should an administrator ever equivocate? While philosophical justifications are difficult to come by, political ones can be bought by the dozen. Is a hyperkinetic professional life a necessity to which one must succumb or a temptation one should resist? Most are tempted and upon occa-

142

sion most succumb. And, so it goes, not only throughout a discussion of the myths above, but throughout any discussion of all other myths crouched and ready to spring upon unwary presidents, vice-presidents and deans alike.

In an intended sense, this book is a story. Its moral is double layered: layer one, myths that are examined closely may yield insights into a complex metier; layer two, stories that are purported to end all stories may not be worth reading.

Index